BEYOND THE FRAME,
BEYOND FEAR

BEYOND THE FRAME, BEYOND FEAR

The Extraordinary Life of Cinematographer
Deepak Haldankar

AS TOLD TO
Dhruvee Haldankar

Vitasta

Thank you for choosing a Vitasta book. For years we've been committed to publishing books that inform, inspire, and endure. Reach out to us for bulk purchases at preeti.vitasta@gmail.com
Discover more titles at www vitastapublishing.com

Published by
Renu Kaul Verma
Vitasta Publishing Pvt Ltd
4348/4C, Ansari Road, Daryaganj
New Delhi-110 002
info@vitastapublishing.com

ISBN: 978-93-47098-32-1

First Edition 2026
MRP ₹ 595

Edited by Soham Debsarkar
Typeset by Shubhpreet Kaur
Cover Design by Smriti Maheshwari
Printed by Vikas Computer and Printers, New Delhi

Contents

Advance Praise

After the interview he said, 'Should I now take closeups?'
Me: Ok, if you want!
Trying to save my 1:3 ratio of film stock!
A camera person whose lens was ever in focus: on attention, intuition, empathy.

-Meera Dewan
Filmmaker and columnist

Cinematographer with a unique sense of visuals—he could visualise things, humans, movements even before the directors could show him the story boards. He was Mother Nature's son and a daredevil indeed. Working with him as a director was a real treat!

-Rama Pandey
Film and theatre personality

Deepak Haldankar was literally larger than life and this personal account penned by his daughter, Dhruvee, does justice to that remarkable life.

- Siddharth Kak
Indian television producer and presenter

My First film *Mundan* was shot by Deepak—his sensitive photography brought the story to life, and our friendship deepened as I discovered his humility and kindness. A true artist with a heart that spoke through his lens, Deepak Haldankar was a master documentary filmmaker. I'm delighted his daughter Dhruvee is sharing his legacy through this book—a fitting tribute to a remarkable photographer and human being.

-Ila Arun
Indian actress and TV personality

Deepak Haldankar with his wit and humour matched any company. His knowledge of the film world was wide and extensive deserving great merit. I have personally known Deepak for 25 years and can vouch for his total integrity in the film world.

-Sharawati Prabhu
Indian mountaineer

Deepak Haldankar was a true lensman—endowed with an extraordinary ability to capture the perfect moment with the right angle, lighting, and cinematic effect, and present it with striking visual clarity.

He possessed an energetic, well-balanced personality. His expressive gaze was so captivating that it felt as though his eyes were playfully interacting with the camera lens.

He had an exceptional speed and discipline in covering events—an ability that seemed to speak for itself. His control over moments and emotions made his work stand out with quiet intensity.

Deepak Haldankar arrived on the battlefield of life like a warrior, clad in his own protective armour, carrying his craft with artistic grandeur. His attire and demeanour reflected a readiness to cross turbulent rivers, effortlessly drawing the attention of ordinary people.

He was a rare and a remarkable lensman.

Today, as I turn the pages of the past after so many years, I vividly remember Deepak Haldankar's confident smile. Salutations a hundred times over to that unforgettable karma-yogi.

-Virendra Mishra

Former Editor, DD-Urdu

I have seen him working with dedication. He always took up challenges whatsoever, maybe the condition. He was ever ready to take shots in extreme conditions. A successful man indeed.

-F A Waris

Chief Recordist, Films Division of India

If you want to learn from the life and work of the reputed cinematographer, Deepak Haldankar, in the areas of technical skills; being one with lights, camera and composition; artistic vision, creative thinking, adventurism and much more, then this book is for you.

-Anoop Kumar

Executive Director (retd) ONGC

A brilliant cinematographer with an artist's eye whose lens captured not just images but the soul of the world. His travels spanned continents—from the serene Himalayas to the icy-majesty of Antarctica. A true connoisseur of life, he found joy in flavours often turning simple meals into delightful feasts. To me, he celebrated the art of 'Live Life King Size' to the fullest!

-Praveen Mathur

Executive Director (retd), Catering Chefair Flight,
Catering-Hotel Corporation of India

His deep knowledge of photography and the intricacies of camerawork always fascinated me and I found the stories from his travels around the world with Presidents and Prime Ministers thoroughly enjoyable and enlightening.

-Nitin Mathur
Director (retd), IT oprerations,
Cap Gemini Systems

My brother, always more than a filmmaker, voice of emotion—capturing life, love, and meaning through his lens.

-Ravi Kiran Haldankar
Younger brother

Always a hero, Uncle Deepak's legacy lives on, inspiring generations to chase horizons, conquer peaks, and capture life's breathtaking moments.

-Dhruv Anand Haldankar
Nephew

Foreword

Right at the outset, on behalf of every reader of this compelling book, let me thank Deepak's talented and entrepreneurial daughter, Dhruvee for bringing to us this extraordinary tale of her courageous cinematographer father.

'Life mein kuchhh Karne-ka hai...' was a recurring refrain and a one-line philosophy of my childhood buddy Deepak, with whom I played a daily shouting match of challenges and promises, on the way to and from my school. Looking back, I realise that our friendship was a bit of a mystery, as we studied in different schools and were temperamentally distinct. Probably, it was because Deepak, like me, wasn't given to mindless, repetitive and noisy games that other boys played—in spite of his athletic build. Or perhaps, I secretly envied the quiet confidence he shared with his father, with whom he would sit on the steps of their ground-floor apartment, watching the world go by, neither cowed nor intimidated by the shadows of elders that loomed over most of us.

We had two things in common: we lived on the same side of the road, and we were both crazy about films. And what tremendous luck! Andheri (the Mumbai suburb we lived in) was a veritable centre of film production! Within a one-kilometer stretch, five major studios hummed with activity. Thanks to his healthy aversion to fear, he led our clandestine 'sorties' into these forbidden kingdoms of thrill.

On our first outing, I froze at the sight of burly Pathans guarding the gates of glamour and who seemed to only acknowledge large cars and garishly dressed humans. But Deepak was Deepak. He had a plan to surmount the barrier all worked out: *'Dekh, kuchh wrong nahin kiya toh darne-ka nahin.'* Instead of begging for entry, he coolly asked for the Production Manager, saying that we are new 'spot boys', and are already late for the shoot. We must have looked like boys from good families fallen on hard days! We sailed in!

Once inside, we weren't interested in the stars. We were captivated by the mechanics. While others chased autographs, we observed the choreography of light and shadow—the camera gliding on a trolley, the director's whispered instructions, and the cinematographer's sharp commands: *'Baby ka pet kaato!' 'Bhandor (Barn door) thoda band karo!' 'Solar par paper lagao!'*

It is now a part of film folklore that during one such secret mission, Deepak sneaked onto the legendary Sheesh Mahal set of *Mughal-e-Azam* at Mohan Studios. He stealthily tiptoed to the viewfinder for a glimpse of the famous dazzle, was caught, and promptly thrown out. A couple of decades later, he met that same legendary cinematographer—not as an intruder, but as an established professional.

As the years passed, our paths diverged into our respective destinies. I watched from afar as he navigated the 'struggle' of feature films, working with masters on landmark projects. But then came the pivot. He decided to switch to documentaries!

When I questioned this unusual swap, his steely resolve came to the fore: 'In feature films, the farthest I can go is to become an ace cinematographer. In documentaries, the whole world will be writing the stories, and I will be the one to capture them.'

And then a matter of 'shame'!? Oh well, he had made a hard-hitting, bold documentary entitled *Mala Laaz waatat naahi* ('I am not ashamed'). True to his impulsive nature, he issued a telephonic order from, guess where, my studio, *"Jaldi se aa-ja, ek emergency recording karni hai!"* That recording led to a rare National Award for me, but equally importantly, it renewed the bond between two old friends. It filled the communication vacuum of years and stayed with us until the very end.

Suffice it to say, 'Adventure, thy name is Deepak Haldankar.'

Deepak, *tune toh life mein bahut kuchh kar-ke dikhaya re...* (You really did show the world what you were capable of).

Love you, my friend.

Harish Bhimani
Indian artist and writer

The Fabric of a Dream

Scaling mountains on my own, fighting battles—professional and against nature—with unwavering resolve and emerging victorious against the odds!

Who do you think I am?

Am I an average John Doe, or am I Deepak Raghunath Haldankar?

I am writing because I wish to tell the future generation that 'Legends Are Not Born—They Are Forged in Fire.'

Read it as a story or use it to find a war cry within yourself and dare to dream beyond the limits imposed by people surrounding you, and most importantly, beyond the shackles of your own limiting thoughts.

This is for every young person or artist standing at the edge of uncertainty, wondering if they have what it takes. For every warrior, who has fought their battles alone, bruised and broken, but has carried on with reckless but gay abandon, and walked away stronger.

I present to you the story of a man who defied fate. Who captured history, braved riots, danced with death in the frozen wastelands of Antarctica, and soared above the world—both in love and in art.

Cameras may capture moments, but some moments capture 'you'. This is my story, and I write it not to recount the past, but to set fire to the future.

To the dreamers, the outcasts, the rebels—this is proof that you, too, can carve your name into history.

So, let's hold hands as I take you down my memory lane.

The scent of fresh green chickpeas and roasted corncob filled the air as the crowd cheered under the bright sun, watching cricket matches with unwavering enthusiasm. Among the players was my father, Raghunath Shambhaji Haldankar—a government employee, but more than that, a Ranji Trophy player, a stylish opening batsman, a sharp wicketkeeper, and an avid photographer. His charisma was undeniable; wherever he went, laughter and energy followed.

My earliest memories of him are how he always entered the room with a burst of energy and laughter and won everyone's heart just with the way he spoke.

As a child, I idolised and imitated him to the T. The way he spoke, dressed, walked, ate, and combed his curly hair—all of it. When he would put white shaving cream on his dark skin, to my eyes, he seemed like some dark-skinned, curly-haired Roman king, maybe Septimius Severus.

In his absence, I would step into his polish-perfect shoes and stand tall, mimicking his every move.

His sense of adventure and wanderlust was my guiding force, my beacon, my Pharos. He pursued photography as a hobby, capturing moments with an artistry that fascinated me. It was in those early years that I unknowingly inherited the love for the lens. Art was in my blood; after all, I hailed from Haldona, a small village in Goa known for producing several prominent personalities.

Born in 1947 in Dharwad, I spent my childhood in Belgaum, studied at St Xavier Church School, and lived in a home surrounded by vast open grounds.

My mother, Chaya Devi Haldankar, was a woman of strength. With a childhood shaped by her father, a forest officer, she grew up surrounded by animals. Her home was a sanctuary for dogs, cats, hens, and even deer. My younger brother, Ravikiran—fondly called Kinna—was my mother's favourite, but together, we admired our father's effortless mastery of both cricket and photography.

When my father was transferred to Mumbai for work, she raised us—her two boys—alone, imposing no-nonsense and strict rules, but ensuring that we never lost our sense of adventure. It was here in Belgaum where we were introduced to the evening *shakha* by Mohan Bhagwat a little further ahead of my school. The RSS officially explains the concept of *shakha* as 'a saffron flag that flutters in the midst of an open playground, and youths and boys engage in varieties of indigenous games.' There are also exercises and singing of patriotic songs; and all activities are totally disciplined. Generally, the evening *shakha* is meant for students and the younger lot, while the morning *shakha* is meant for relatively older people, who may not find time in the evening to attend the *shakha*.

Belgaum was my playground. My best friends—the Balaji brothers, Ashok, Prakash, Subsha, and Mohan—and the Kundarkar brothers, Annu, Suresh, and Vasant—shared countless adventures with me. We spun tops, played *gilli danda* (tipcat), and flicked marbles that glistened like tiny orbs of art. My father taught us how to craft kites, and coat the *manjha* (strings) with finely powdered glass and glue—a deadly art to turn a simple thread into a sharp cutting weapon.

The glue to mend the kites was always in short supply because of our meagre budget. So, I used to jump across the wall into the veterinary hospital opposite to my house, nick a stem off the drumstick trees, and collect its sticky sap to replace the glue for mending torn kites.

My childhood was all fun.

Undeclared and unexplained, my father was leaving impressions on my naïve, but very curious mind. I was like a little girl chasing butterflies in the garden, lots of them, in many colours and hues, in many shapes and sizes, coming and going, rushing past me.

The only difference was that the butterflies were all the mechanical miracles happening around me, and I was not a dainty girl, but this dark, not yet tall, handsome, 'hungry-for-more' boy.

One day, a car pulled up and out stepped three men, The Malshet Brothers, and holding intricate aero models, entered a nearby ground. I wanted to see how these aeroplanes were taking off and landing just exactly like real aero planes.

Enthralled, I ran to my father. 'Papa! Will you take me to see these aeroplanes closely?' I asked enthusiastically.

As the miniature planes soared and landed with precision, he explained the *modus operandi* of how the fuel mixture of petrol and castor oil powered the engines. That moment ignited my love for mechanics and movement.

Be it the sky or the ground—my curiosity was getting fired up from all around me. One day, a huge roller on the road had drawn my attention. Before that, I had only seen hand-pulled rollers on the cricket field. With a sparkle in my eyes, I followed it to the road construction going on at the end of the road. Papa started taking me for his matches from Belgaum to Dharwad, travelling by trains. The smoke-chugging steam engine, pulling so many huge carriages, brought my heart to my mouth. I would press my face against the window, mesmerised by the rhythmic chug of the locomotive and the ever-changing landscape. Little did I know that this fascination with motion would one day define my life's work.

We would often visit my grandfather and other family in Dharwad, a city of goldsmiths. My grandfather, a man of precision and discipline, owned a factory manufacturing medical instruments.

'Deepak, would you like to come with me to the factory?' my grandfather would ask, and I would jump up and accompany him to the factory near the Belgaum Forest and watch with a gaping mouth as surgical tools took shape under skilled hands. These visits sowed the seeds of my appreciation for craftsmanship and attention to detail.

My young mind had another influence—my cousin brother Daulat Mutkekar, who studied in Lingraj College, known for its excellence in fine arts and dramatics. Daulat Dada was also actively involved in the college cultural committee and politics at that time.

One day, he sweet talked me into canvassing for his student body election. Like an obedient soldier, I set out to ask each person encountered on my rounds.

Imagine—as a little five-year-old, I entered a graduate classroom where the professor was writing on the board. I stood on the desk and shouted on top of my voice, 'Vote for Daulat Mutkekar.' There was a lot of commotion. All the students laughed, clapped and enjoyed the disruption from a boring lecture.

Needless to say, the teacher caught me by my ear and escorted me out of the room.

To my utter dismay, I also received my first reprimand from Papa.

I felt stupid, but for some reason, I did not feel bad about helping Daulat Dada. After all, he was an accomplished playwright, dramatist, and a budding politician, and I looked up to him too.

Much later in life, I realised that he was my first window to the world of stagecraft and creative productions.

Unwittingly, life in Belgaum was providing the cogs and bolts for my future.

Its rich tapestry of marvellous unfolding of man, nature and machines, quirky friendships, cheeky mischiefs, and astounding discoveries were going to shape my wheel of life.

Soon, a new chapter awaited us in Mumbai.

Mumbai is a very strange city, as it never sleeps, but gives and shapes numerous dreams of its inhabitants!

A City of Sleepless Dreams

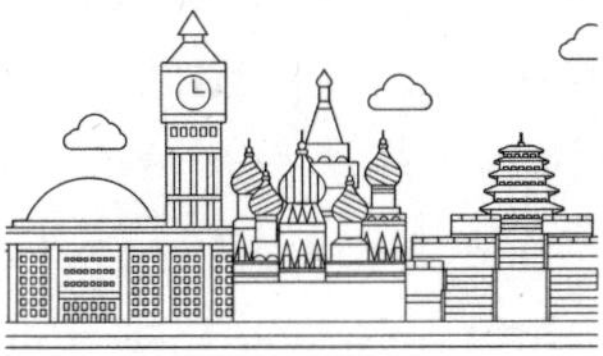

Moving to Mumbai was like stepping into an entirely new world. The bustling streets, the towering buildings, and the ceaseless energy were overwhelming yet exhilarating. We settled in Andheri, a neighbourhood with a rich history, and a landmark that fascinated me, especially the rarest of rare Gilbert Hill, a prehistoric volcanic formation—a single slab of vertical rocks hundreds of feet in length, standing tall amidst the urban sprawl. Soon our family of four had a very new entry, my youngest brother—Anand. There was a huge age difference between me and him, but that did not deter me from loving him wholeheartedly. Papa loved all three and called us his rare and precious gems!

I got enrolled in Holy Family School. With the architectural expansion of Andheri, my school got shifted to Mahakali Caves Road from the Andheri Kurla Road. This new location was also beautifully surrounded with mango and cashew trees and had paddy fields nearby. Most importantly, I could pass by Prakash Studio, Modern Studio, Mohan Studio, and Manoranjan Studio (M&T) on my way to school. I quickly found my place, excelling in dramatics, elocution, and sports. My curiosity extended beyond textbooks—I was drawn to the science of light, sound, and motion. I was a sharp observer and a keen learner, and wanted to recreate the things I saw, understand their mechanics, and make them my own. Chemical compositions, measuring light and sound, stars and constellations always fascinated me.

My cheekiness found a partner in a charming, suave, English-speaking fellow called Roy D'abreao.

With a naughty plan in mind but unsure about him, I asked Roy, 'Roy, will you agree and decide to make a bomb with me?'

'What do we have to do, Deepak?' Roy asked inquisitively, much to my delight.

'To make a bomb with a long fuse, we need explosives,' I replied.

Roy looked at me pensively.

'It's Diwali time, and lots of explosives will be available easily.'

I was the mastermind, and with clear authority, I said, 'But we have to be sure and have to be present in the classroom when it explodes.'

And so, after a few undercover test runs, the D-day came. Everyone in the school heard a sudden loud blast. Many students were questioned, including us, but we were in our classroom with forty other students, and our teacher stood witness to that.

We succeeded in making and blowing up a bomb on our own and escaped being caught, giving us a wrong sense of achievement. But it did one good thing, i.e., Roy and I became very good buddies, there for each other through thick and thin, and someone with whom I could share my deepest secrets and plans for the future.

Those who walked the halls with us will forever walk in our hearts; friendships born in school are pure and untainted. I was a worthy friend not just to Roy, but also to Naresh Sharma, and Ajit Khatri. Ajit was a year senior to us, but we gelled so very well. I loved watching English movies, and it was such an ordeal to travel all the way to the town side where these movies were screened in Eros, Regal, New Empire and Rex Cinemas. We would watch two movies a day, from 12 noon to 3 pm, and from 3 pm to 6 pm. The English movies did not last for three hours, so we would have enough time to have snacks and travel from one movie theatre to another. Naresh's father was a famous still photographer in the film industry and had a darkroom and film processing laboratory at his residence. On weekends, when Naresh's dad would be travelling, we would rush there and learn about the film developing process.

Generally, we live our lives without any major impact, but we never know which day will hold what for us, right?

I also had a rendezvous with my destiny one fine day, just like that!

One bright sunny day in December, Papa took me, Mummy and Kinna to see a film shooting at Modern Studio. The film was titled *Police*, starring Pradeep Kumar and Madhubala, and they were filming a song. Both the actors were lying on a bullock cart stacked with hay. The cart was placed in front of a big screen where the scenery behind moved. The Mitchell Camera was mounted on a crane. Suddenly, I heard a shout: 'Full lights, start sound, roll camera, clap, and action!' This was the first time I had heard these commands and their execution. Papa got busy in explaining the nitty-gritty of what was happening around us, with as much photography knowledge as he had. He said that this technique was called Back Projection. As I looked at him, I could hardly hear him, but I could see the aura he carried, coming from a family of artists, singers, and painters.

As I turned around to see the workings in the studio, I knew in that moment that this is where I BELONG. My bread, my butter, my jam, my beer, my work satisfaction, my accolades, my reason to get up in the morning—all will come from THIS art field.

From that moment on, I became a silent observer in Mumbai's film studios. Skipping school, I sneaked past compound walls to witness history being made. In 1958, I found myself inside Modern Studio, where *Mughal-e-Azam* was being filmed. The grand Sheesh Mahal set sparkled under the lights, its shimmering reflections creating an illusion of endless depth. I tiptoed towards the camera, lifted the black cloth draped over it, and placed my eye on the viewfinder. Just as I did, a firm hand pulled me back.

'*Tere* school *ka time ho gaya hai, chal bhag yaha se,*' said the man, barely hiding his amusement.

That man was R D Mathur, the legendary cinematographer of *Mughal-e-Azam*. Years later, when I had carved my own path in the world of cinematography, I met him again. When I reminded him of that day, he laughed and asked, '*Aur aaj kal kya kar rahe ho,* Deepak?'

'I am a cinematographer, sir,' I replied with pride.

***

One frame at a time, my life had taken me to the place where I could confidently call myself a cinematographer.

The journey ahead was filled with struggles, triumphs, and moments that would shape my life.

Mumbai was a city with a whirlwind of possibilities, and I was determined to carve my own path. My passion for cinematography was growing, but I knew breaking into the industry would not be easy. Unlike others who had a smooth entry, I had no godfather, no guiding hand—only my relentless ambition and the fire in my heart.

My early days were spent working as an assistant cameraman, absorbing every detail, learning from masters of the craft. I assisted great cinematographers like Nariman A Irani, Joe D'Souza, and Anwar Siraj. Each film set was a battlefield where I fought to prove myself, pushing beyond exhaustion, waiting for my moment to shine.

I watched *Pakeezah* being shot in M&T Studios, and even got a chance to assist Nariman A Irani who completed the film. It had taken fifteen years, and about twenty-five cinematographers worked on the film to complete it. Cinematographers like Jal Mistri, Arvind Lad, D K Prabhakar were all a part of the film, however, only Josef Wirsching's name appeared in the credits. Nariman A Irani taught me the art of cinematography, and became my guru. *Pakeezah* was shot using a cinemascope lens from Metro-Goldwyn-Mayer. In those days, I used a Latter (German camera) 35 mm ARRIFLEX BL with a 400-feet magazine, and later switched to an SR 16 mm ARRIFLEX camera. I worked with Anwar Siraj, Joe D'souza, Dara Engineer, Keki Mistry, Roengton, and many others to learn their techniques, but my major source of inspiration and knowledge remained Nariman Irani.

One of my proudest moments came when I saw my name in the credits for the first time. It was a Konkani film, featuring Shalini Mardolkar in *Moji Gorcan*, directed by the legendary A Salam and photographed by Joe D'Souza in the beauteous lands of Goa and Baroda. The movie was also special because it was shot aboard a ship called *Rohini Choughole* Shipping Line, and my school friend Inder was the deck officer on that ship.

That connection got us all the VIP treatment. And when we reached the location, Shalini Mardolkar and A Salaam were staying at this majestic bungalow owned by Mr Mannuel. I was surprised to be greeted by my classmate Beena at the bungalow.

'Deepak! What the hell are you doing here? So nice to see you!' she said.

Beena was Shalini Mardolkar's sister and instantly recognised me.

'I am assisting Joe D'souza!' I replied with confidence.

My status in the unit was elevated. The film was completed in two schedules. Lawrence Pereira, the son of Mr Pereira, president of the then makeup artist association, joined the second schedule. I had begun making connections in the film industry, and was enjoying the process thoroughly. All this hard work had started paying off, and I finally got my membership for the Western Indian Cinematographers Association–Junior Grade 2–764.

I was now a legitimate filmmaker.

Standing in the dark cinema hall, watching my name appear on the screen, I felt an overwhelming sense of triumph. It was proof that I was no longer just an observer—I was a part of the magic.

I climbed the ranks, project after project, proving myself through sheer grit. Soon, I became a cinematographer in my own right, known for my eye for detail and ability to capture raw emotion. The camera became an extension of my soul, a medium through which I could immortalise the stories of others while scripting my own.

The Third Eye—My Camera Lens

My association with Nariman A Irani gave me a glimpse of the world of mainstream commercial cinema. But joining the films division was a turning point in my career. Here, I was no longer just a cameraman—I was a storyteller, capturing the essence of India's evolving history. The organisation was established in 1948 to maintain a record of Indian history on celluloid, and joining them in their 24, Peddar Road office, I became an important cog in that wheel. I filmed momentous events, travelling across the country, capturing footage that would become part of the nation's visual archives. But in my wildest of dreams, I had not imagined that one day I would work with the world-famous Italian director Michelangelo Antonioni. He came to India to shoot the famous Maha Kumbh *mela,* and I became the first Indian cameraman to shoot as part of his team.

I found a lot of inspiration in his work style; for example, I found that he freely creates his raw stock, without any spot cuttings. He would shoot whatever he saw; and later sit down to edit, which was different from what I had learned, i.e., shoot with a lot of precaution and brevity. But seeing him, I realised that this was a much better way, as you did not have to make an on-the-spot decision of what to keep and what not. The chances of missing out on so much raw stock was reduced to minimum.

I also worked with S Sukhdev, who was famous for his pioneering approach to documentary filmmaking addressing social issues and known for his stylistic choices, such as the use of handheld cameras.

It was an auspicious day of Dussehra in Ludhiana. I was an associate with Sukhdev *ji,* who was working on the film project titled *Sukhirama.* It was a multi-screen film with a CinemaScope multivision projection on seven screens. A cinemascope 35 mm screen is where 1+7 images are projected in a special dome theatre with a large hemispherical screen to create an immersive visual experience.

At 6 am in the morning, before getting in the car, he said, 'Deepak, from now on, you will take over, as I have to urgently leave for Bombay for editing. You will continue filming in Srinagar, Rajasthan, Punjab and Haryana.' I was thrilled to hear this.

'I believe you will be able to handle the CinemaScope camera well,' he said to me while others in the crew ogled.

My calibre was being recognised, and my joy was boundless. The film was shot with one CinemaScope camera with an ultra-scope lens and other cameras simultaneously, all cameras being 35mm ARRIFLEX.

One of my most significant initial films was *The Flying Sikh, Milkha Singh*, which I filmed in 1970. It was the story of a frontrunner from Chandigarh who used to run so fast that it felt as if he was flying, and it turned out to be the start of my flying career.

As I stepped on the soil of Chandigarh, I felt transported

to a different land—neat and clean. I reached his house as the breezy wind touched me, with the sweet smell of blooming mango, guava, and eucalyptus, fragrant with neem trees. It was 8 am, and his daughters Mona and Aleeza were playing in the garden. Their loud, uncontrollable and infectious giggles mixed with the sweet smell that filled the air. It got me thinking that this is how heaven must feel like!

My trance was broken when I heard Milkha Singh saying, 'Hello! *Namaste*, you all must be the team from the Films Division.'

'Welcome, welcome. I am going for *shikar* (hunting). Would you like to accompany me? You can do your shooting, while I do mine, hahaha!'

'Oh yes, sir! Shooting with a camera is my profession, but I would love to try your style of shooting as well,' I replied jokingly.

We chatted like old friends, and I told him how I practised shooting guns for a hobby, and always loved watching Gregory Peck, Sean Connery, Terence Hills, and Jayne Eastwood films with gun-fighting scenes. In fact, Jayne and I shared the same date of birth as well.

That day we returned tired, but jubilant from hunting three well-camouflaged and swift partridges. Milkha Singh was an expert hunter.

The next day, I started the shooting—I mean with a lens, dear friend!

We were almost wrapping up when Milkha Singh invited me and my team for dinner.

'Deepak! *Yaara, kal saath khana khake jaayin* (please have dinner with us tomorrow),' he said in Punjabi.

'Sure, Sir, will do, thank you,' I said, graciously accepting the offer.

The next day, I arrived with my team, and was lovingly welcomed by his wife, Nirmal ji, who was laying the dinner table.

Durga, who was Milkha Singh's close friend and the then chief of the Films Division in Punjab, was also present.

'I have heard you completed the film, Deepak,' he said, smiling.

'Oh yes! I did. This film will be the first-ever film shot on Milkha Singh Sir. There will be many more to come, but this one will remain the first!' I smiled with pride.

The film took seventeen days to shoot, and had enough footage to showcase Milkha Singh's relentless spirit as the honest, simple, jovial but disciplined man that he was, totally dedicated to his sport.

It wasn't just a documentary—it was a tribute to perseverance, to speed, and to a well-balanced, cultured life.

With *The Flying Sikh, Milkha Singh,* my confidence started building.

One day, I was asked to assist a senior cameraman, Vijay Parmar, for a film in Ladakh titled *Arming the Mountains,* a film on the defence of the mountains, directed by S P Ganguly. We all reached Ladakh on a cloudless summer morning. I was very excited, as Vijay Parmar was a well-known name in the industry, and I was looking forward to learning a lot from him. As we stepped out of the airfield, Parmar felt a strong pain in his chest and had to be rushed to a nearby hospital. The director S P Ganguly got very stressed, not only for his health, but also about what to do now.

He asked me with some trepidation, '*Kya tum khud yeh kar sakogey,* Deepak? (Will you be able to do this on your own?)'

I didn't even have to think for a response. '*Mai yahi kar sakta hun, sir!'* I replied.

And I shot the film to the full satisfaction of S P Ganguly and applause from the public.

I had started doing good films with the Films Division. One day, I got an interview call from Pramod Pati's office. He was a documentary film director, an animator, the chief of Films Division, a big name, or rather a pillar of the Films Division. I reached Gulshan building in Bombay (Mumbai), which is a museum now.

I will be honest—seeing around twenty-two candidates sitting there was very daunting.

But I waited for my turn, with my head held high.

When my name was called, I went in and saw M M Vaidya, the chief cameraman; Abhyankar, the administrative officer; Acharya, the admin assistant, and a few more distinguished people staring at me. To the right side of the table, was a SIKI 35 mm camera, and on the other side was an ARRIFLEX 35 mm camera.

One of them said, 'Please have a seat and introduce yourself.'

This was easy. I spoke with assertion.

'Hello everyone, my name is Deepak Raghunath Haldankar. I am a cinematographer. I have assisted cinematographer Shri Nariman A Irani, and have done films like, *Pakeeza* starring Rajkumar and Meena Kumari, *Don,* starring Amitabh Bachchan, Zeenat Aman and Helen, *Talash,* starring Rajendra Kumar, Sharmila Tagore, with O P Ralhan as the producer and director, *Balidaan,* starring Manoj Kumar and Saira Bano, and *Maharaja,* starring Sanjay Khan, Nutan, and directed by Naresh Sehgal. I have also worked with the cinematographer Anwar Siraj in three films —*Victoria 203, Yakeen,* and *Do Bhai,* and also *Dara Engineer.*

'Apart from that, I also worked with Joe D'souza

for the film *Mojhi Ghorkan* starring Shalini Mardolkar, Jasian Vaj and directed by A Salaam.

'I am also a junior member of the WICA, Number 764.'

Without any acknowledgement, they asked, 'Have you seen a frame when a car or a horse carriage moves from left to right and the wheels move in the opposite direction? What's the effect called?' M M Vaidya asked sternly.

I confidently replied, 'Stroboscopic effect!'

There was silence in the room.

'Have you worked on this camera?' he asked, pointing at the SIKI camera.

'Yes, I have, sir,' I replied.

'It is a copy of Mitchell and is not reliable, as the polarity changes and the camera gets choked,' I added.

I could feel a palpable wave of surprise passing across the board members.

'Can you thread film in it?' he asked.

'Yes, of course, sir,' I replied and showed them how it was done. Just then, they asked me if I had worked on an ARRIFLEX camera. I said with my cheeky smile, 'I know the camera well.'

'Load the magazine and thread it,' one of them said.

I loaded the magazine perfectly. In addition, they also asked me about colour temperature, depth of focus, filters, and other questions—all of which I replied with confidence.

Pramod Pati's smile was a giveaway of how impressed he was by my answers.

'When can you join, Deepak?' he asked.

'I could join this very moment, sir,' I jibed.

They told me that I had cleared the UPSC Exam but would have to go to the Patna office.

'You're not happy? Why are you still here?' asked Mr Pramod Pati.

'Sir, please post me to a station where my calibre is made good use of,' I told him politely.

He paused for a moment, thought, and said, 'I will post you to Delhi on one condition: that you rush to Delhi immediately.'

In an hour's time my orders were revised, and I left Mumbai the next day to join the Films Division office in Delhi as a Newsreel Officer.

I, a small-town boy, jumped states and boundaries with a camera on my shoulder in search of new captures through a third eye—my camera lens!

On 26 February, 1974, I met Pramod Pati again at the Films Division office, smartly dressed and sharp as ever. I can never forget him and that UPSC interview.

He said with a smile, 'How are you, Deepak?'

I said, 'Very fine, Sir. And thank you once again.'

'Oh, you deserve it, young man. But never let me down,' he said, tapping my shoulder.

I would do a lot of weekly coverages and had become quite popular among my colleagues. My seniors, Prem Vaidya, who was the director of the Camera Department, and M M Vaidya, my UPSC Exam panel member, and the chief cameraman at Films Division, were my superiors, and I loved working around them.

One day, it was 4:30 pm, and I was preparing to leave the office when my boss, M M Vaidya called me and said, 'Haldankar, you are required to accompany Prem Vaidya with a talkie camera and sound unit. Start preparing and just talk to him if he requires anything else.'

I immediately called Prem Vaidya, who instructed me to reach Ravindra Natya Mandir at 6:30 pm with all necessary staff and equipment. He said, 'We will leave for the location from there.' I had no clue about the assignment.

We reached the location and entered the theatre, where the army troop was rehearsing.

'Fix the camera; I will join you later,' he said.

I placed the camera tripod at 90 degrees in the aisle centre to the stage in the third row of the seating arrangements. The sound engineer took the line out from the stage console. We were ready and watched the rehearsal. It struck me then that I had been assigned to cover the prestigious national celebrations of 15 August.

Prem Vaidya came back and smiled as he saw my stance, like that of a rampant lion.

Thereafter, he recommended my name for many independent important coverages.

On 15 August 1947, the first Prime Minister of India, Jawaharlal Nehru, raised the Indian national flag above the Lahori Gate of the Red Fort in Delhi. Every year, independent India is celebrated at this historic Red Fort in Old Delhi.

I filmed many exquisite Prime Ministers of India unfurling the national flag and addressing the nation, from Mrs Indira Gandhi to Dr Manmohan Singh. I would stand at a coveted position, just seven feet away from them, with my camera, as the representative of the Films Division of India.

The little patriotic and brazen boy in me was very proud of retaining that position year after year. In my mind, I had decided that I will continue to do this till my last day with the Films Division.

With the numerous films I made for the Films Division, I also won several awards on many occasions. By now, I was conversant in shooting in adverse conditions. Filming fascinated me, and the 35mm Eastman colour film, and the 40 x 90 feet large screen had captivated me.

But since childhood, I was always in search of the next adventure. So, this was a happy place but not enough for me. *Dil mange* more—isn't it?

Bittersweet Memories

I enjoyed working in Delhi, sitting and moving around with high-level politicians and dignitaries, and driving around on my Royal Enfield motorbike. Delhi was much colder than Mumbai or Goa due to its proximity to the Himalayas.

This was the month of December, and I loved the way my strong, sturdy bike forged ahead, tearing through the dense fog of December in Delhi, also the month of my birth. With my curious, energetic, and 'hungry for more' Sagittarius instincts, I drove to my office on Pandara Road.

It was a very beautiful ride, passing through a very posh residential area called Khan Market, with huge *jamun* (Indian blackberry) trees, laden with juicy black *jamuns* and bougainvillaea flower shrubs on both sides of the road.

Oh my god! What a variety of colours—multiple shades of baby pink, coral pink, flamingo, and fuchsia, red, and white, luxuriously spread across the walls! The roads had a canopy of greenery, and I drove through it on my motorbike—the roar of a full throttle, the throaty growl of the twin piston engines, and the thrumpy exhaust notes of a vintage classic—*vroom vroom vroom!*

Let me tell you a secret that I never told anyone—sitting on my Enfield, I used to feel like Maharana Pratap sitting on his horse Chetak!

Delhi fascinated me with all the gates it opened up for me, with a camera on my shoulder and adventure in my heart. In those days, the camera used to be quite heavy and big, and carrying it around had created a dent on my shoulder. But that didn't bother me. I was happy making, directing and photographing outstanding films with outstanding people.

One day, I reached the office and saw a very attractive, dusky-looking woman having a conversation with the chief producer.

As I approached, he introduced her to me, 'Deepak, meet Rama Pandey. She is an actor, writer, and director, and she is here to produce a film for the Agriculture and Irrigation Ministry.'

He continued, 'Rama *ji*, meet Deepak Haldankar. He is the chief newsreel officer and an ace cinematographer.'

We exchanged pleasantries, and immediately I started asking questions about the agricultural film project, like how, when, where, and expressed my happiness to join the project. I was already researching and had made a few films on issues which could be brought to the people associated with agrarian India. It was an educational film about agricultural field publicity, about how to build better farm homes with good use of home science and hygiene. Rama had written a very colourful, interesting song and drama script, which she planned to direct herself, and was happy to take me on as the cinematographer. Rama also acted in the film along with her two sisters, Illa Arun and Tripti Pandey, and brother Prasoon Pandey.

We went to Naila Haveli in Jaipur, and the trio of girls looked stunning. The Rajasthani dresses, heavy silver jewellery, and their agile body frames were such an eye-catcher. The three girls and I became instant friends.

Don't get me wrong, the men looked great too in their colourful Rajasthani *pagdis* (headwear).

The shooting started, but by now, I had realised that work was not the only thing I loved. I was also a sucker for high-class and tasty food.

'Deepak, why are you always hungry,' Rama asked jokingly.

'*Bhuke pet na hoye bhajan Gopala!* (No one can work his best on an empty stomach!) I am thirsty for orange juice and some onion *kachoris.* Please send out a spot boy to the Jaipur market,' I replied, laughing.

'Yes sir, why not! *Aap kahey to dastarkhaan lagwa dun*!' Rama was known for her sharp retorts, but it was all in good humour.

So, I carried on with my shots. The film was shot on 16 mm colour film, and it was titled *Mundan.*

Even though the film was an educational motion picture, I shot it in cinemascope with a good scale to enhance the beauty of live song and dance sequences that Rama and Illa did during the scenes. During the course of the film, I also clicked still pictures of these beautiful women. Multiple shots in succession on a film camera being my speciality.

This was Illa Arun's first tryst with a camera, and I was the one behind it. Needless to say, there were many, many more to come, as I could see how brilliant and crisp she was, as an actor and singer.

***

This film in Rajasthan was all dance, colours and fun, and I enjoyed every aspect of it. But I had to return to the Films Division doing documentaries. My adventurous spirit was raising its head again.

One day, at the Films Division office, there was chaos, and N S Thapa, the chief producer, was pacing up and down the room.

'What's the matter?' I asked.

'Who can go to Bastar?' he asked, flabbergasted.

'A film on Bastar? Is the Films Division doing a film on the Bastar tribes?' I asked, astonished because that tribe is ill-famous for Naxal activities.

N S Thapa looked petrified (as he often did!). He asked me, or rather commanded me:

'Haldankar, will you go to Bastar district to film the people living in the periphery of Abujhmad?' he said and pointed at the map behind him on the wall.

'We need to film the people living there. It's an ancient land covering 2,200 square kilometres, in the forest area, where about 14,000 people live in almost complete isolation from the outside world.'

'Tell me, will you, would you? No questions asked, I know you will! I know you are brave and will not say no for an answer.'

As if he had decided for me, and he would not take no for an answer!

But I agreed to the proposal and started packing for Chhattisgarh, Madhya Pradesh, because I wanted to do challenging films. I wanted to climb the mountains and dive under the sea. What the heck, I wanted to do an expedition every year! And this was as dangerous as an expedition.

I reached and totally immersed myself in the lives of the Bastar tribe. Hiding from the local authorities' strict and fearing eyes, I developed a mutual trust and bonhomie with the tribe. I even changed the way I dressed up. Initially they were apprehensive, but soon my friendly demeanour, honest toothy smile, my short *langot* (loincloth) draped in their style, my curly dark hair, my dark skin, my strong muscular physique and my ability to drop all inhibitions and eat what they were eating broke that wall of doubt, and they let me into their inner circle. I could meet and talk to the women, children and the older people. Needless to say, I maintained perfect discipline and did not do anything to anger them.

Their local name was *Abhujhmadi* tribe, and their lifestyle was astonishingly open, democratic and what we can call 'modern'. Their women draped a long cloth around their bodies as their dress with no stitches. They were not overly conscious of their bodies, especially the sex organs. Touching on shoulders by strangers was not allowed, as it was perceived as an attack. I filmed unmarried girls and boys spending a night together to choose their partners for life. Sex among them was free within their codes of conduct, as young boys and girls could spend the nights together. But it was not to be used frivolously. It was to marry and extend the tribe.

How romantic and modern and so different from the place we call modern civilisation!

The favourite pastime for the boys was cockfights. Possessing a good fighting cock was a symbol of prestige among the men. Filming a cockfight was one of the many highlights of my film. The section was called *A Call to Ghotul* as *ghotul* was the communal ground used for training and cockfighting.

The *Abhujhmadis* brewed their own liquor with their traditional techniques and ingredients. But it was not consumed frivolously, but only on special occasions like weddings or festivals.

Again, how modern, healthy and safe for the community!

Abhujmad meant the 'unknown hills', and I got a perfect title for my film, *Where Time Stands Still.* It was a very revolutionary film showcasing the life of a primitive tribe clad in mystery.

It won an award.

On 24 March 1978, the film was released and won an international award at the Bilbao, Leipzig and Warsaw Film Festivals.

Amidst all the accolades and pats on the back, I felt the same exuberance as I had felt when I had done the impossible task of jumping over the walls of famous studios.

I always knew I was brave, but now the world was acknowledging that I was brave—that was fun. I just became hungry for more chances to show my adventures to the world. The adventures that they would die for!

On 13 August 1980, a rumour spread that a stray animal had entered the Eidgah on the day of Eid-al-Fitr prayers. The police were asked to remove the animal, and it led to a heated argument, which eventually led to riots between the Hindus and Muslims in Moradabad, and spread over to other cities like Sambal, Bareilly, and Delhi.

I was asked to film the 1980 Hindu-Muslim riots in Moradabad. Nobody else in the office would come forward for such duties.

Hundreds of civilians were being killed. The official death toll was officially around 289, but unofficially, the toll could be even higher.

The streets were ablaze, communities torn apart by violence, and public property damaged with stone pelting. I filmed amidst the chaos, my camera serving as both a shield and a weapon, capturing truth in its rawest form.

Through my camera's eye, I saw mass destruction and recorded everything with a bitterly heavy heart because as the newsreel officer, I had a huge responsibility to record this horrific news for the world.

'*Iss daadhi waley ka gala kaat dey* (Cut the throat of this bearded man),' a man screamed aloud and came running towards me.

'*Nahi nahi mujhe mat maro, main Musalmaan nahi hun* (No, no, please don't kill me. I am not a Muslim),' I said, begging for mercy. '*Mera naam Deepak Haldankar hai, main Hindu hun* (My name is Deepak Haldankar. I am a Hindu),' I said, showing my government identity card to him.

My goatee beard was my pride and life till it became the reason for a threat to my life!

The man had enough sanity to look at my identity card and let me go.

Later, the government of India's Films Division awarded me for my bravery, and I was the only cameraman to receive this award. But it was at the cost of developing thanatophobia. My sound recordist, Shyam Sundar, felt this death anxiety too for years to come.

However, apart from the award, another good thing that came out of this was my reinforced belief in the power of visual storytelling—sometimes, the world needs to see the truth to change it.

A Love Story in the Sky

Even amidst my relentless pursuit of fame and success, fate had other plans for me.

The Films Division was assigned to cover the International Bookfair held at India Gate. My office boy, Jaguram, prepared my equipment, and off we went.

Those were the days when people of all ages were still drawn to books. Mobile phones, especially smartphones, were not even fathomed. So, the place was bustling with young boys, girls, parents with kids, old people, and all and sundry. Some were browsing books enthusiastically—novels, mysteries, science fiction, comic books, picture books, *et al.*

I was busy as usual, eyeing through my camera and capturing shots, when my eyes fell on two charming girls standing at a counter and looking at cookery books.

One of them spoke in Hindi, 'Cake *bananey ki koi kitab hai kya bhaisahab*? (Is there a book on baking cakes, brother?)'

The cheeky boy in me saw this as a sweet angle for the otherwise boring topic of buying books and asked their permission to take their shots. They asked, surprised, if they were going to be on TV! I said 'yes' and introduced myself.

Sadhana Mathur was a radiant, sweet, attractively sharp-featured woman, with glowing clean skin, and an air of simplicity that drew me in. I instantly fell in love with her long, lustrous hair and sweet talk. She and her friend Sunita Gupta, who accompanied her to the fair, were both studying hotel management. I instantly invited both of them to the Films Division office to watch the film coverage once it was ready at the private theatre inside the Films Division office. I also told them that they could also watch it on *Bhartiya Samachaar Chitra* (Indian News Review).

It was my usual practice to invite my friends and family to the in-house theatre to preview all the films I shot, but these were strangers.

But so what? Adventure was another name for Deepak.

They accepted the offer, and one fine day, they came to my office. Sadhana had a baked orange cake in her hands as a birthday gift. We laughed and recollected how we met at the book fair. I met these lovely ladies quite a few times as we developed a good friendship. We spent time in Lodhi Gardens, had lunches at Pandara Road restaurants, and watched movies at different cinemas around my office. I and Sadhana started talking for a long time on the phone, and one day, Sunita jokingly asked if we had developed some feelings or what!

That innocent comment brought out a thought hidden deep in the heart. Till that time, I was thinking we were just friends, but as I prepared a response for her innocent quip, I realised that 'YES, that was it! I love this beautiful, innocent, pure girl, and I want to marry her and be with her for the rest of my life.' I had found my soulmate, my partner in thick and thin, a happy listener to my adventurous sagas, a patient bearer of my requests, and most importantly, I loved to eat, and she loved to cook! What better alignment can there be!

She was the universe's gift to me. And I would do anything to accept it.

'Wow, Deepak! I can't wait to tell this to Sadhana, but it's better you propose to her, and then I shall speak with her!' Sunita said hurriedly.

I hung up the phone, nodding to myself, gearing up for a grand proposal.

What is life if not a little drama, and this was my proposal to my sweetheart, my Sadhana. It had to be special.

I was the pioneer of aerial filming in India and had done it many times to cover political occasions. I called my pilot friend and told him that we have another aerial mission in about one hour.

He thought it was another government mission, so he said that he had not received any orders. But he sensed the urgency in my voice and came to pick me up. I had called Sadhana and told her to check the skies after one hour. In his helicopter, we went to a location over Sadhana's home, and as we hovered, I dropped rose petals on Sadhana and her mother, asking for her hand in marriage.

'Sadhana, will you marry me, my love?' I screamed out loud from the helicopter.

Before the mother could understand anything, Sadhana's answer to this dramatic proposal was a big 'Yes!'

We got married in a simple Indian wedding on 1 October 1980, and began our journey as husband and wife.

She became my anchor, my greatest supporter, and my partner in all things.

In the fast-paced world of cinematography, she was my calm. While I chased impossible shots and captured fleeting moments, she grounded me, reminding me of the beauty in life's simplest frames.

Rubbing Shoulders with the World's Best

As part of my job, I was often called for high-level political and social functions in India, and accompanying Prime Ministers and Presidents was a regular thing by now.

One day, I got a phone call from Mr Sahai from the Photo Division.

'*Tum shaadi mai ja rahey ho kya?* (Are you going to the wedding?)' He asked eagerly.

'Whose wedding?' I asked.

'Prince Charles *ki shaadi*, yaar. *Dhai hafton se proposal chuppake rakha tha magar* Diana *ne haan kar di hai aur unki shaadi hai* 29th July *ko* (Prince Charles' wedding, my friend. They had kept the proposal a secret for the last two and a half weeks, but Diana has said yes, and they are getting married on 29 July)!' He sounded exasperated, as if she had said 'yes' to him!

'It's too early; I have no information!' I replied.

'I have a friend in London, Dr Ratan Prakash, the President of the local youth organisation. He is extending an invitation for the visiting journalists to spend an evening together. He is with me on the phone right now, so please talk to him,' he said.

It was too big a deal—going to a royal wedding in the UK, and getting invited to royal dinners. I was not thinking on my feet. 'I am not sure if I will be included in the delegation, Mr Ratan, but thank you very much for thinking about me,' I said to him.

'Nevertheless, I am extending an invitation to you, Deepak. Please do visit me when you come to London,' he said, sounding as if he had made up his mind.

The next day, I learnt that I was accompanying our President, Shri Sanjeeva Reddy (the sixth President of India) to the wedding. I still remember it was 9.30 am on a Wednesday morning, and I was feeling euphoric reading the government letter. I asked if I could take my wife along, a newlywed bride and a princess in her own right!

I was denied respectfully, as there were many guests, so there was a strict headcount allowed from each country. My name beamed on 'Prestel', the world's first working view-data portal.

In preparation, I grabbed as much data as I could on Great Britain, on the couple, and on the royal family to set some perspective on the things I wanted to cover. Sadhana was a bit disappointed, but she understood my helplessness.

We were in our married bliss, with me telling her all the nitty-gritty of the wedding information, and she was helping me with my travel planning. Her cooking was too good to be true. Everything that she cooked had a special taste and aroma: her vegetable stew, her biryani, her spinach *paneer* curry, her mutton *pulao*, her chutneys and her sorbets.

Guys, I can go on and on and on— somebody please stop me!

She was my *Grih Lakshmi* (the home goddess). I was truly blessed, as she managed my idiosyncrasies, my quirky behaviour and my home. Like this one time, when returning from Assam,

I got five huge jackfruits in a sack.

She exclaimed, '*Hum bas do hi toh log hain. Aadhe se bhi kam chal jata, aur tum panch uthaa laye* (We are just two people! Just half of a jackfruit would have been enough, and you have brought five big ones)!'

I had nothing to say, so I just hugged and kissed her, saying that I know you will turn all of these into delicious food. It was indeed bothersome for her, but she was really good at it.

This was my regular—getting things in bulk. I loved buying, and as a special convoy, there were no weight restrictions for us.

As part of my UK preparation, I got a few tailor-made suits and my usual film gear of 8-pocket jackets to fit in all my filming gadgetry, made by a close friend and a renowned tailor, Rajeev Malhotra. He was the only one who could cater to my strange appetite for clothes.

Can you imagine a bright red suit? I wanted it, he made it, I wore it, and people gasped at first, and then loved it!

But for this royal event, I got two casual corduroy jackets with cravats, and two formal black and blue pin-striped suits with matching shoes, ties and a bow for the D-Day. With a finely trimmed beard and well-combed curly hair, I was not feeling any less than a prince myself—an urban, oriental, lion-hearted prince!

On D-Day, I took my camera position at St Paul's Cathedral. While we all waited for the arrival of the princess, I captured the ambience of the crowd present, waiting eagerly to catch a glimpse of the royal couple. Diana's dress was unique and elegant, covered in thousands of pearls with an exceptionally long trail, and as she came out of the coach, catching her father Earl Spencer's arm, the crowd shrieked in pure ecstasy.

I was behind the camera, capturing all the beautiful shots

and angles. But probably this was the first and last time in my professional life when I felt, for a second, to leave the camera behind and soak in the style, grandiosity and bliss of the moment.

But work is work, and my work was to film the Indian President's presence at the royal wedding, and that is what I did and came back. On my way back, I bought a few kitchen gadgets and gizmos for Sadhana's kitchen.

***

At Chennai College in Mumbai, I used to act in stage shows and theatrical plays like *Aladdin, Alibaba and Forty Thieves*, and Shakespearian plays, and now I was filming documentaries, and rubbing shoulders with great movie personalities. I was constantly learning new techniques and polishing my art.

Air India sponsored an event with Michael Peissel from France to fly to India to showcase the usability of a fan-driven hovercraft he had invented down the river Yamuna from Delhi, reaching Prayagraj, and then all the way up to Gangotri, upstream on the Ganges River.

I was invited to film the expedition with Major D N Das as the liaison officer and Captain Kohli as the main administrator.

Das was from Dehradun, and was well acquainted with the areas of Uttarkashi, Yamuna, and Ganga since his childhood. He was a decorated blue badge holder in the National Defence Academy for his excellence in sports, yacht sailing, and other water sports.

We became good friends, as he exclaimed, 'One pleasant thing that happened in this expedition is that I met you, Deepak!'

Pioneering white water river rafting in India, Major Das

planned an expedition on the river Jamuna by boat, and made a mention to me about this thrilling journey he wanted to execute. He offered me to film it—the Jamuna-81 Rafting Expedition.

I was happy to do it, but it needed to go through the government sanction first. The Ministry of Defence wrote to the Films Division and the Army Adventure Foundation, and they agreed to sponsor the expedition, but with many strict regulations. It was an endurance test for both men and material. Standard reconnaissance boats were to be used as rafts.

The Army Service Corps (ASC) was responsible for the logistics support to the army, navy, air force, and paramilitary soldiers. In all kinds of terrain and at distant places, the ASC provided the armed forces with food, petroleum and transportation. Their task was very challenging, making the ASC very daring. This expedition was to take a break from their routine work to experience water adventure.

We took off on 12 September. To carry eight team members, four pneumatic rafts, each for two people were made. There were risks all along the way—cross currents, quicksand, whirlpools, water snakes, and more. We crossed the famed Sikh shrine of Ponta Sahib and reached Delhi, 425 kms away, on 29 September.

Yamuna–81 was to become the frontrunner for the next bigger Ganga-82 Expedition, and I successfully shot a film on water adventure.

Ganga-82 was an even more thrilling adventure. Major Das wanted this expedition to be a great memory for the participants. He welcomed their spouses to get on board too. We started the expedition on 16 March 1982. After a week's training, the courageous men set off from Uttarkashi, and Sadhana happily and fearlessly came along.

My coy civilian wife was shoulder-to-shoulder with the wives of the army personnel.

The expedition went on its way, camping on the banks in tents at night, and drifting on the river, by day. The journey sometimes went smoothly, and sometimes turned rough.

The task of a cameraman is a lonely one, as everybody is on the other side of the equipment.

As a lone ranger, I had to search and take positions, like a hunter, to pick the right angles and wait patiently for the action. As I was sitting on this side of the lens, waiting for the right shots, two rubber rafts collided with each other, and someone fell in the water.

Everyone screamed, '*Arre! Rassi pheko* (Oh, throw in the rope), help help.'

I sat, filming the entire incident as Major Das and Lieutenant Puri went up and down in the water after colliding with Major Mohan and Major Biley's raft.

I was wearing my photographer's hat so tightly that I forgot to respond as a fellow rafter. My only thought at that moment was that this shot must be captured in its entirety.

The team refrained from talking to me for the full nine days, as they were upset with me. They thought that I should have left everything behind and at least thrown a rope since I was the nearest.

But, how could I?

By 29 March, we had had a few more accidents on that trip. But no life was lost, and Sadhana and I were safe.

My team had reached Devprayag and were sitting on the Ganga's shore near a dense jungle when we heard the news that another raft had been lost. The water current was very strong, and the riverside had lots of pebbles, rocks, and thorny bushes. I was alone but decided to help, and gathered a couple of civilians and policemen to search for the stranded members. I carried some blankets, candles, water bottles and some medicines.

It was around 6.30 pm, and the sun had set, making the place darker than usual.

We had walked about 5-7 km, when I saw a pair of burning red dots right in front of me! When I heard some noise, I realised that it was a cheetah, growling and waiting for the right moment to pounce. There was no escape route—a river with icy cold water was on one side and thorny bushes on the other side. And death incarnate was in front of us!

I couldn't think of anything to do, so I started screaming at the top of my voice. The cheetah, who was advancing, stopped, and as he stopped, the others started screaming as well.

The sub-inspector lit a matchstick, pulled off the *lungi* (sarong) of a civilian next to him, and put it on fire, and hailed it like a flag. The fire changed the cheetah's mind, and he pulled back and ran away in the other direction.

We resumed our search, and after nearly two hours of arduous ordeal, we reached a cave and found our team there.

Courage was the expedition's motto, and everybody was displaying their mettle.

In my enthusiasm to shoot from uncommon angles, I slipped from a rock, and fell into the swirling waters while shooting the confluence of the Bhagirati and Alaknanda rivers and the origins of the Ganga.

My first concern was to save my camera that hung around my neck. Tightly holding onto the sturdy stem of a tree, I watched in despair, my raw film reels and other equipment wash away.

The locals who had assembled to see the shooting rushed

and pulled me up. Within an hour, I revived my spirits and started my work again.

On 7 April 1982, the expedition came to an end. The film was titled *A Tale of Adventure – Ganga-82.*

I was pleased at being able to successfully film the 207 km-long adventurous journey of nine brave men, negotiating the turbulent waters of the river Ganga, and Sadhana vowed to accompany me again, if possible.

Conquering the Frozen Frontier

One day, Krishna Kumar Garg, the deputy chief producer at the Films Division, asked, 'How are you, Deepak?' We were walking into the spacious Films Division's raw stock room where I was to arrange my equipment on the shelves.

'*Kya Jadoo kiya hai tumne* Mrs Indira Gandhi *par* (What magic have you done on Mrs Indira Gandhi)? *Jab dekho tumhara naam hi leti rehti hai!* (She is constantly mentioning you!)'

Just then N S Thapa entered the room and joined in the conversation.

'K K is right, Deepak! Madam Gandhi specially called me and specifically told me that I want only Deepak to accompany me on my tours!' he said sheepishly.

My first tour with Mrs Indira Gandhi took me to Iraq in 1974. She became very fond of me, and I found her to be a very strong woman, and felt pride in accompanying her.

That's when I shot the film *A Day with the Prime Minister Indira Gandhi*.

I looked at K K Garg and asked, 'Has madam recommended me on another tour?'

Just then the phone rang, and I walked to my cabin to answer it.

'Hello, I am Dalvi speaking. I am the PA to the Secretary of Oceanography; you are invited for lunch at 1.00 pm,' he said.

'Yes, thank you! But why am I invited?' I asked.

'I am not aware of that, but can you please reach 10 Pandara Road,' he said.

I was surprised because that was my own office address.

He paused for a bit and corrected himself. 'Sorry, it's 10 AB Pandara Road. And please also bring along your biodata,' he added.

'Sure, I will,' I replied and hung up, immediately after which I left for home. I showered, changed and reached the address I was given.

When I arrived, I saw a garden umbrella and buffet tables laid and a handsome man wearing a sleek suit walking on the lawn.

'Hello there! Sir, I am Deepak Haldankar,' I walked in, introducing myself.

I didn't realise, but 'Hello there' had kind of become my usual way of introducing myself, like a *takia kalam* (a catchphrase).

'Oh, it's you!' He looked at me surprised. 'Please come, you're welcome!'

We sat down, and he asked me, 'You must be wondering why I have invited you?'

'I wanted to see who you are in person because your recommendation is coming directly from the Prime Minister, Mrs Indira Gandhi!'

I felt ecstatic. 'Why am I called?' I asked curiously.

'Have you heard of Antarctica,' he enquired.

'Yes! Of course,' I replied.

'There is going to be an expedition. The team is not

modulated yet, but you are the first member induced into the team,' he said.

I was so thrilled and surprised to know this. I conversed with him at length, and he asked me to keep it a secret.

'It's top secret; don't even mention this to your wife yet, and start preparations now,' he advised.

He was Syed Zahoor Qasim, the Secretary of the Oceanography Department, a noted Indian marine biologist, and a very humble, well-spoken man.

He is the one who advised Mrs Indira Gandhi to have a camp station in Antarctica, describing the importance of the frozen continent of India as the only place where the Indian Ocean meets with the Antarctic waters, being closed by landmasses and the Himalayas towards the north.

Keen to follow in the footsteps of her father, Jawaharlal Nehru, and committed to the international order, Indira Gandhi planned this expedition to showcase India as a growing power before all major global multilateral forums. It was a secretive mission with only three other officials in the loop: Krishna Swami Rao Sahib, the cabinet secretary; K Saigal, the additional cabinet secretary and also the former member for the intelligence committee; and Ram Sathe, the foreign secretary.

Under her guidance, India began formulating its strategies for Antarctica during the same time when the United Nations convention was finalising the laws of the sea. With a young team of scientists drawn from seven different research institutions, Operation Gangotri was born, and India started its first Antarctica expedition in December 1981.

Sathe selected Dr Qasim to lead this mission. With the treaty of 1991 in place, stating that the onus and responsibility of all decisions and actions in the future will fall on experts with prior experience in matters related to Antarctica, Dr Qasim went on the first mission, on 9 January 1982, but he was not accompanied by any cameraman or videographer. But for the second round, it was decided to have a cameraman onboard. And I was the chosen one!

It was *The Antartica Expedition 1982-83.*

The expedition was led by V K Raina, the Director of the Geological Survey of India, with experts from eleven different disciplines like geophysics, microbiology, meteorology, and zoology, besides other streams. Studies were to be conducted in bacteriology and virology, as well as the physiological and psychological pressure connected with living in isolated conditions in extremely low temperatures. For India, the Antarctic region was of special significance because the weather pattern of the Indian Ocean was closely related to conditions in Antarctica.

Most of the equipment required for the expedition was made in India. For example, the communication equipment was supplied by Bharat Electronics Ltd and Marine Communication Equipment Ltd. Dehydrated food was supplied by the defence Food Research Laboratory and the Central Food Technology Research Institute.

The two prefabricated shelters were constructed by the Central Building Research Institute at Roorkee, built as strong shelters with specially treated wooden blocks lined with asbestos and covered with thermocol for providing insulation from cold, with a lining of corrugated zinc to protect it from the onslaught of blizzards and cold winds for housing staff and scientific equipment. The camping equipment was supplied by the High-Altitude Warfare School and the Indian Ordnance Factories. In addition, two caterpillars and two additional snow-scooters were imported for work on the landmass.

Despite preparing in-house equipment and material, the everyday expenditure of the expedition was very high for the government—about Rs 1 cr a day!

I was responsible for filming all the scientists in action, capturing all the big and small details as they worked out a way to set up a permanent site for future expeditions.

For our initial training, we were transported to the High-Altitude Warfare School at Gulmarg, Jammu & Kashmir, and Drass, one of the world's coldest places to inhabit. It had an altitude-influenced Mediterranean continental climate, with an average winter temperature at around -20 degrees Celsius which would easily drop to as low as -23 degrees Celsius at the height of winters. In summer, the average temperature is close to 23 degrees Celsius (74 degrees Fahrenheit).

At Drass, I received training on many survival techniques such as fieldcraft, icecraft, self-survival, radio procedures, and living in field huts, and only after passing them was I taken on the Antarctica expedition.

On 27 November 1982 at 11.00 pm, after an initial team conference with the team leader Dr Raina, I arrived at the room I was allotted. The room was not as comfortable as my earlier foreign stays at posh 7-star hotels, or the room that I was allotted with Sadhana during the earlier expedition with Major Das. It was a guest house near the NIO (National Institute of Oceanography) building in Goa. This place had an eerie silence to it. I quickly went off to sleep, as conserving energy was very important.

The NIO was a huge building with a lot of commotion, and had a number of people working in their fields of expertise. This is where there were hundreds of samples from the ocean beds collected for experiments. I also saw corals, like the ones I had got from Lakshadweep on my last visit with the Prime Minister.

Earlier in the day, I also went to the nearby harbour, the Dona Paula Point, where Mrs Indira Gandhi had visited, with her personal physician Dr Mathur. We had gone for a boat ride and spoken on many general topics.

The following day, I went to the ship anchored nearby to do some filming. It had arrived much earlier than expected. It was a Canadian ship called *The Polar Circle Ice-Breaker*, a 500-tonne vessel that was linked to its control room back home with the help of satellites.

It had two naval helicopters, and a specially trained crew. Goa is such a beautiful place. I recollected I was here about fourteen years ago on an assignment during the same month and had stayed till January. I celebrated my twentieth birthday in Goa. This time, perhaps, I was scheduled to be in Mauritius on this ship, and on to the coldest land on my birthday on 17 December. It was also the year the Asian games were being held in India.

Four days later, I had begun the 10,000 km journey from Goa to Antarctica. It was a twenty-eight member expedition team, along with a fourteen-member crew. We started the journey from Goa on 1 December 1982, and the expedition left with eleven truckloads of equipment. I had packed along with me twenty-two suitcases, containing my camera equipment, my camera for motion picture, ARRIFLEX 2C and Nikon for stills, my personal belongings and lots of food items, like pickles and munchies. I was prepared mentally, physically and emotionally, and had studied my equipment well.

I knew my camera ARRIFLEX 2C very well, and could repair it myself, if needed. All the equipment was treated with special anti-fog grease, and subjected to rugged tests. Above all, I carried with me one most important item I could really take for granted—the Eastman colour negative film Type-5247, with all my worries regarding equipment and visual judgement under such harsh conditions. I depended a great deal upon the physical powers and exposure latitude of 5247 and was sure it would prove me right.

We took an unusual route through the Indian Ocean and had to pass through the turbulent oceans and a 'Desert of Ice' before making the successful landing.

This expedition, I must say, was desirable, for not only adding to national prestige, but also for its value for scientific exploration.

'Antarctica held the master key to the history of the Earth,' with that, I started my shooting spree.

Antarctica as a continent overwhelmed me, as it was larger than the USA and Mexico combined, or India and China put together. Ninety per cent of its area was covered with ice, estimated to be 1.5 to 2 km thick, locking up within itself, 90 per cent of the freshwater resources of the world.

The frozen continent was an unforgiving land—with temperatures plummeting to - 88 degrees Celsius, and blizzards that roared like beasts. Every step was a battle against the elements. Yet, standing amidst that endless white expanse, I felt invincible. I had conquered yet another frontier.

Our first halt was at the port in Mauritius for a technical checkup, inspecting technical specifications. The crew changed here to further continue the journey to Antarctica.

On 19 December 1982, the *Polar Circle* crossed the 40 degrees south latitude that separates the warm waters of the Indian Ocean from the cold waters of the Arctic. The ship had passed the confluence of the Indian and the Atlantic oceans, which were very rough. The landing of the ship was done after helicopters had undertaken extensive reconnaissance.

The base camp was set up 4 km from the site where the ship was anchored. As per international conventions, a prefabricated refuge hut was set up. The equipment was also installed without mishaps.

Experiencing six months of day and six months of night, our expedition lasted 110 days with 24 hours of daylight. I worked for 18 hours a day.

The light was constant, and the sun travelled in a straight line 40 degrees over my head. The continent was one of the stormiest and windiest places on earth. During summer, the temperature ranged from -15 to -20 degrees Celsius, and during winter, from -50 to -88 degrees Celsius.

To put it in perspective, let's take an example. In a normal place like Delhi or Mumbai, at a speed of 60 km per hour, a tree could bend from one side of the road to the other side.

Now, think of clouds and wind passing at a speed of 300 km per hour in Antarctica!

We were trained to keep ourselves warm and in efficient working conditions to such extreme degrees.

There were moments of peril. Yet, I emerged, stronger than before, with a story that could be told for generations.

The footage I captured became a visual testament to human resilience, a record of mankind's ceaseless hunger to explore the unknown. A journey that made India stand tall before the world.

One morning on a breezy day, I left the camp and started walking. Since the earth is round, even after walking a long distance, I could not see a static point. Rather, all I could see was a curve. I didn't realise, but I had walked almost 30 to 40 km! Feeling extremely tired, I felt sleepy, and dozed off instantly.

I was missed at the base, and my team realised that I was gone for a long time. Everyone wondered where I could have gone or if I was lost.

Two helicopters were sent to look for me. They hovered for many kilometres and could not locate me.

I was reported missing to Mrs Indira Gandhi, and as per the protocol, my team members waited for a signal from her.

'Search one last time thoroughly,' she ordered the high-frequency radio transmitter that was assembled at the site for direct communication with India.

The helicopter took off one last time with Major Jay Vardhan Bahuguna sincerely hoping to find me. He was a leading mountaineer of India and an Indian army officer with the corps of engineers.

Fortunately, he had a sharp eye and saw me as a red dot at a distance on the white ground. He jumped out with 2 men and walked towards me only to find me sleeping peacefully. I had been fast asleep for over twelve long hours!

'Wake up! Deepak,' he said, shaking me awake. 'What the hell are you doing here?'

'Do you know you've been missing for more than twelve hours! Get up now, let's go,' he yelled into my ears.

'Who's going to bring my camera?' I asked him.

'Get going. We will bring it!' he screamed.

I was brought back to the camp and checked for any medical impact. I was then strictly reprimanded for forgetting the basic rules taught in the training. I was never to venture out like that again by myself and that I should always have company.

Mrs Indira Gandhi was informed, and she breathed a sigh of relief.

Embarrassed at all the mayhem I had caused, I jokingly

mentioned that I could be in the Guinness Book of World Records for sleeping in Antarctica for over twelve hours at a stretch wearing just a red coarse jacket but with a cravet—I did not want to be remembered for not working and sleeping like Indians do in government offices. I laughed.

This adventure had left me very hungry, so I asked John, our cook, if I could get some curd-rice, which was our staple there, along with ice cream.

I loved eating ice cream in Antarctica and if allowed, I could just finish the whole slab in one sitting!

'There is very little curd left, Deepak; just one last cup is left. We have to wait for the supplies to arrive,' he said. 'Why don't you eat something else,' he suggested.

Always the experimental type, and having learnt from my mother when she used to make us sit next to her as she did her kitchen chores, I suggested, 'I could help you make some fresh curd if you permit me.'

To his surprise, I took a lukewarm barrel of milk, added the one cup of the leftover curd to it and set the temperature of the incubator to 36 degrees Celsius.

'Chef, let's wait for three hours, and I shall hold my hunger,' I mentioned to him.

After 3 hours, the curd was so well set that I could cut off a slice of curd with a knife like a cake. The wait was long, but I enjoyed my meal of curd-rice with fresh homemade curd.

John was so happy and impressed that he gave me the permission to enter the kitchen on the ship any time I wanted. It was a rare privilege given to anyone from the team, as the chef was very territorial, and would not allow anyone inside his domain.

***

It was another cold morning in Antarctica. We landed two helicopters at the Wolton mountain, rising to about 1,450 metres in height, to collect samples and specimens, while I filmed the beauty of the mountain glaciers.

Once they finished and were ready to fly back, we realised that the first helicopter was not taking off.

Captain Gill suggested that we take the other helicopter and bring back help to repair the first. I, along with Captain V K Raina, took off in the helicopter to bring help and reached the advance camp—a facility that supports scientific research in the region. We had to stop here, as the helicopter had to refuel because we had travelled a long distance, exhausting all the fuel, and the base camp was still about 200 km away.

The crew started refuelling, and a lot of fuel had already been loaded when I observed something and screamed. I noticed that the fuel being refilled was of the wrong variety. The fuel meant for snow scooters was inadvertently getting refuelled into the helicopter.

'It's the wrong fuel in the tank. The helicopter will explode on take-off!' I shouted out loud, alerting the naval pilot.

The pilot heard me and immediately clammed up. He looked at the barrel, then looked at me, stunned. Once again he looked at the barrel and shivered with fear.

'Stop! Stop refuelling!' he shouted. The fuel was stopped then pulled out. The tank was cleaned by rinsing the tank 3-4 times, and fresh fuel was finally refilled in the tank.

'How did you know that wrong fuel was being filled, Deepak?' the pilot asked me. He was very curious.

'Well, I had filmed fuel loading in aircraft like the Antonov AN12, Sukhoi, on some earlier expedition, and one careful look at the fuel barrel made me realise that this was not the right one. Also, as a child, I used to read a lot of books on aircraft and helicopters.'

I was happy that my love for gathering information and my keen eye for detail had come in handy.

***

On a funny note, let me share another minor difficulty that every expedition goer faces. The continent of Antarctica is five times larger than China, with about 5,000 scientists present at any given time, with an ice sheet covering almost 14-million square kilometres, so huge that if it melts, the world's oceans will rise by 50 metres.

There were teams from Russia, East Germany, and America, and all worked with cooperation. Especially at the time of strong blizzards, they extended full cooperation to each other in extreme situations. For example, I remember once, an East German vehicle got lost, and was traced by Indian helicopters. Or the teams from all countries joined the Indian team to celebrate Republic Day on 26 January. That day we all liberally exchanged films and food.

But all had to devise their own ways to attend to nature's calls. A layman cannot imagine how difficult going to the loo was in this place!

I developed my own system for peeing, as I would keep the skidoo (ice scooter) switched on and wait for the warm heat emission in my direction, and only then release myself!

Otherwise, you can well imagine what one would get—a gelid, frozen stream! Funny to the onlooker, but extremely painful for the bearer.

***

Every expert group had their own objectives and priorities, and we remained loyally committed to them.

My priority was to complete the film for the Department of Ocean Development—a 35 mm colour documentary recording every minute detail of India's second expedition to Antarctica. However, for the scientists, the priority was to set up a station in as short a time as possible, and in that sense, the presence of a cameraman could have been a disturbance. So, many times, our objectives got in the way of each other. So, I had to cajole and convince the scientists about my presence in their faces, as it was very important and pertinent to capture their discussion and actions.

With this attitude of 'I must do what I must do', I will share another story.

Once, it was a summer day in Antarctica, about to melt into the evening. The sky was very beautiful and bright, with winds blowing at a comfortable speed. I was taking different shots from different angles, and my gaze reached up ahead on the sea surface. I wanted to take a pan shot of the *Polar Circle* cutting through the ice and moving smoothly. So, I decided to position myself at a spot where I could best capture the moving ship, which meant getting off my own ship and stepping on an ice glacier, mounting myself and equipment at a position with a clear view of the ship. The glacier was very huge, akin probably to the size of a multi-storey building.

I announced to Captain Raina, 'Sir, I am getting off the ship to take a very important shot. It may even become the opening shot for our film.'

I was lost in my own thoughts and visions about how I would take that shot.

'No, Deepak, I cannot allow you to do this stunt. Can't you

see? It is a huge risk,' said Captain Raina.

I started arguing and persuading him, as I believed I was the master of my trade. How could Captain Raina know how important this shot was!

As we kept talking for about 2-3 minutes, the captain moved his head in a way that meant he was asking me to turn around and see.

'What?' I retorted, on being interrupted.

I turned around and saw the glacier quietly submerging and disappearing into the sea.

I stood dumbfounded, just as the captain stood horrified.

'Look, I just saved your life, Mr Deepak,' he said with relief.

'I am sorry, Captain, I shall listen to you from now on,' I said, breathing a sigh of relief that there was someone around like my father, who could look beyond my histrionics.

***

I had exposed 150 rolls of Eastman colour 35mm of 400 feet, 200 still rolls, 200 rolls of colour Kodak negative, and 200 rolls of Ektachrome film by now.

I am not sure whether Antarctica was more dangerous or more beautiful!

Imagine, there are more than sixty-three species of birds who live exclusively in Antarctica, like kelp gulls, light-mantled albatrosses, white-chinned petrels, the fierce and feathered skuas, Arctic terns, and king penguins.

What majestic strides, what smooth flights! It was a treat to the eyes and the soul.

For the first time, the penguins must have tasted Indian food in Antarctica. Initially, they spat it out, but eventually, they started liking it, and gladly accepted *chapatis* (Indian bread) and other food from my hands. They were very friendly birds, and visited the camp and scientific installations regularly. I would spend hours with them, and they learnt to pose for me! Their shrieks and noises also had a method and synchrony to them.

I captured how the scientists collected water samples from icebergs and lakes in special bottles and tagged the penguins to study their life cycles.

Our ship anchored at the Mormugao Harbour on 20 March 1983, and we were welcomed by the Chief Minister Pratap Singh Rane. Mrs Meher Moos, the first Indian woman to set foot on Antarctica, was also present to greet everyone. It was a huge honour and a very warm welcome.

Many women came from neighbouring government offices along with schoolchildren and some senior officers from the three wings of defence. The women welcomed us with *arti* (religious welcoming ceremony) and garlands. Many schoolchildren who had come sang welcome songs. The wives of some members had travelled by road to be present when the ship anchored, and their loved ones set foot on home soil once again. It was emotional to see them hugging their partners. I missed Sadhana very much. But she could not have accompanied me.

This film on Antarctica, entitled *Exploration Antarctica,* won an award at the Maritime Film Festival in France. I got international acclaim for my extraordinary filming skills, including a special mention in the National Film Festival in 1987. But the film did not win the national award because in 1987, adventure photography did not exist as a separate category. But I was ecstatic as I became the first Indian cinematographer to film in Antarctica.

At my home, another form of history was being created.

Since Sadhana was expecting, and it was sure that I would be in Antarctica at the time of delivery, we had already decided that if she delivers a boy, we would name him *Dhruv* because the Hindi name for the Antarctic is *Dakshin Dhruv*, or 'the South Pole Star'. If a girl is born, she would be called *Dhruvee.*

Dhruvee Raghunath Haldankar was born in Delhi, amidst the warmth of her grandparents, her mother, and full medical care. But inheriting her dad's histrionics, she received a name reflecting the iconic expedition undertaken by her father in the most inaccessible, coldest, windiest, and remotest part of the world.

A Legacy in Frames

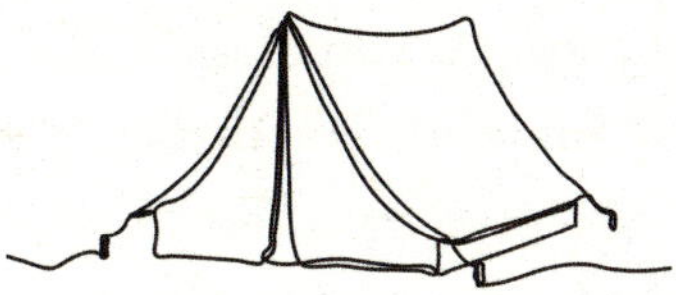

Decades passed, and my journey continued. I filmed history, travelled across continents, and lived a life most could only dream of. But through it all, one truth remained—my camera was more than just a tool. It was my third eye, my weapon, my companion.

I scaled mountains, crossed seas, and faced beauty and cruelty in both life and nature. But in the end, every frame I captured, every moment I preserved, was a testament to the battles I had won.

My lens did not just document history; it became history.

Since I mentioned cruelty, I remember a film of mine *Gift of Love - Case Studies of Two Dowry Victims.*

This probably was the first time when I got accolades, but they were not as tasty and zestful as awards should be. This film won eleven international awards at leading festivals. It won the Silver Peacock National Award, and international awards at Spain, Oberhausen, Cracow, Leipzig, Bilbao, and Cannes.

My film was based on burning brides for dowry—and for bringing the truth to the world of why dowry spelled death.

Meera Dewan, a freelance director and scriptwriter at that time, approached me with the concept. Later on, she directed many more award-winning documentaries on topics like equality for women, children, and the environment.

We both felt deeply for this serious social concern, and I agreed immediately to film it. Dying and killing in the name of dowry were quite rampant those days. We chose two real-life case studies for the film, both on burning brides for dowry.

Facing nature as a force was different, I guess, because even though nature's wrath is very dangerous, it can be managed with proper safety measures and pre-planning.

I had faced some inexplicable human wrath too, in the shape of riots. But the forces I was going to face this time were totally beyond me. How could someone set a living being on fire? And that too, for the sake of some money! And that too— someone who would take your family line forward, if given a chance!

How could you?

Humans are more difficult to understand and manage, and we had to approach this topic with extreme precautions, as any wrong step could disrupt the legal system.

We had taken permission from the authorities and got a call from Safdarjung Hospital, Delhi, that a lady has been brought in with 80 per cent burns and the police are waiting to record her dying declaration statement. I reached the site and placed myself precariously close but not too close to the victim, who was writhing in pain. Watching her shivering body with saline drip wires jutting out from the sides, and hearing her pained voice from under a covered canopy shook me to my core!

She said that her husband, mother-in-law, and sister-in-law had put her on fire! They were asking for a scooter, fridge, and one lakh in cash, which her family could not afford!

I agree that poverty is a curse and pushes people to extremes, but does a curse give anyone a right to become a devil?

I could not sleep for many nights. I could not look into my camera for a few days, fearing what I might see on the other side!

The other case study was a woman from Mathura, who was burned by her own husband, a Bata shoe company employee. He had set his wife on fire, but before that he had called her parents shouting. '*Apna kooda waapis lekar jao* (take your garbage back),' as she was unable to fulfil his needs and demands.

Meera and I decided to visit the woman's family in Lajpat Nagar, Delhi, a rather posh area.

To our shock, the mother served us with a very lavish spread of food, as if it was a happy occasion. The girl's father sat for the interview and shared that they had given everything the groom had demanded, but his demands were never-ending. He often said that they were very rich, and had told the groom in the beginning itself that he will get whatever he wanted; he just had to name it. But they didn't know why he was not happy.

It was weird how the family kept looking at the camera many times and asking when this film would be shown on TV.

Me and Meera wondered that if even after that grim event, they are showing off blatantly with this vulgar display of money, then what must they have been like earlier?

Were they one of the contributing factors for the demonic greed of the groom? They were demanding sympathy now but also wanted to know when they will appear on screen!

They were confused as to why they did not stop the marriage when the groom first demanded it. Rather, they were happy fulfilling his demands, making it seem like a natural thing.

I will never know because I am no psychologist nor police officer nor judge.

I was just a mere man with a lens to watch through!

I felt so small that day, probably for the first time.

So many films are made in mainstream cinema; I was, however, open to capturing stories that the world would see from a different perspective. Stories that would make my audience both laugh and cry. Stories that would show the reality and bring them close to the truth of life. My film spoke a thousand words of the women who lost their lives to burns and ashes.

The film was completed, but its transmission had to stop as the victims' parents pulled off. The accused, with a prejudiced mind, created a ruckus, stating the matter was still subjudice. The Janwadi Mahila Samiti stood strong with us, but it was ultimately withdrawn.

***

Life must go on.... My job was to go from one project to another, one topic to another.

This time, Mount Everest beckoned me. Inspired by the success of reaching Nanda Devi, the second highest mountain in India, in 1984, the Indian Mountaineering Federation (IMF) planned to send a mixed team of men and women up to the peak of Everest.

The world had already tasted huge success when Tensing Norgay, a Nepalese Sherpa, and Edmund Hillary, a New Zealander, reached the summit of Mount Everest on 29 May 1953. After that, Captain Mohan Singh Kohli, an Indian Navy officer and mountaineer, led Indian expeditions in 1960, 1962 and 1965.

The peak eluded them by 700 feet in 1960, and then by 400 feet in 1962, only encouraging them to put greater efforts in future. As a result, the 1965 Indian Everest expedition led by Captain Kohli saw nine men reach the summit of Mt Everest, creating a world record for seventeen years.

Fifteen years later, in the 1980s, the IMF proposed to send Indian women up there, and 1984 saw India's first women on Mt Everest's summit.

I was sitting comfortably, slouched on my office chair, when the phone rang.

'Hello there! Deepak here,' I said.

'Hello Deepak, I am Siddharth Kak. I am a documentary maker and a television producer. I believe you have been to Antarctica and have great experience in filming in cold-bound regions,' he said.

With a twinkle in my eyes and a faint smile hidden in my beard, I replied. 'Yes, sure, that's me. How can I help you?'

'I am making a documentary on the 1984 Mt Everest expedition, and I'd like you to work for me.' He didn't ask. He just declared whatever was in his mind.

'Mt Everest? Who would not want to experience the top of the world?' I was already sold on the idea.

'Oh lovely, I would be interested in the project,' I replied promptly.

My name was once again proposed by Mrs Indira Gandhi. This expedition was part of her vision for Indian women to emerge victorious in all spheres.

We used to meet while covering her official tours, but she never shared that she was forwarding my name. She had a certain clandestine and sassy nature, but in a good-natured way. But she never hid her fondness for me and my professionalism.

'Deepak Haldankar, you must accompany me on all my tours!' Indira Gandhi had proclaimed.

I covered most of her events—in Bahrain, Prague, Czechoslovakia, Spain, Madrid, Maldives, Sri Lanka, Bangladesh, Qatar, etc.

Mrs Indira Gandhi would always take personal interest in viewing her travel footage and the shots I took of her. She was very particular about how she dressed, talked and walked when addressing the nation. I would make it a point to show her a copy of the film personally, especially the close-up shots.

After all, who does not want to look good on screen?

I remember one rainy day in the Andaman and Nicobar Islands. It suddenly started to rain heavily. Mrs Gandhi stepped back inside her car and saw me as I stood ready with my camera to take her pictures.

'Deepak, let the rain stop; step into the car with me!' she said while rolling her car window down. She signalled the special protection group chief to let me in.

I smiled and quickly sneaked into her car.

'Deepak, please don't click me from my profile; I don't like it much. I would like to be clicked from the front,' she confided.

I knew exactly how much she trusted me when she said that.

'Got it, madam,' I said and made a quick mental note.

'I am going to climb Mt Everest,' I said naively, referring to the expedition that I would soon be a part of.

'I know,' she said with a happy heart, and wished me luck.

This iconic expedition was sponsored by the Sports Authority of India (SAI) with a ministerial grant of Rupees 35 lakhs, under her authority.

The film on Everest was going to be produced by TOMCO, as Siddharth Kak was an ex–employee, and a high-quality film producer.

My goal was to create a video that could transport viewers

to the summit of Mount Everest, capturing the climbers, especially the strong Indian women who strongly believed in their own potential.

Mrs Gandhi's aim was to inspire a new generation of adventurers. So, the responsibility on my shoulders was huge and history-making.

After inviting volunteers and nominations from various mountaineering clubs in the country, seventy mountaineers were selected on merit to undergo training in three camps-cum-pre-Everest expeditions to Kabru Dome, Gangotri, and Mana Peak in 1982–83.

Finally, twenty people, including the leader Darshan Kumar Khullar, were selected for the Everest team by the sponsoring committee.

The seven women members selected for the team were Sharawati Prabhu, Chandra Prabha Aitwal, Harshwanti Bisht, Rita Gombu Mahwah, Rekha Sharma, Meena Agarwal, and Bachendari Pal.

The film crew consisted of the director, Siddharth Kak, videographer and mountaineer Sanjeev Saith, sound recordist Nand Kumar, and me. All the members were summoned to Delhi in November 1983 for preparations.

The women, during this period, underwent strenuous training in jogging, swimming, and working out at the National Stadium and spent a month in Gulmarg to get high-altitude and cold-weather conditioning.

They were also sent for meteorological training to observe and record various broadcast parameters at D G Observatories. This was necessary for accurate satellite observations and evaluations so that the team could remain informed about the weather, a vital factor on Mt Everest.

According to the plan, we paid home visits to each mountaineer team member to see their daily lives away from the extreme pressure of the expedition and to see who they really were when they were not working, and when they were with their families.

I filmed Bachendari Pal at her house in Nakuri, Uttarakhand. She shared that she was preparing to be a schoolteacher, and mountaineering was elevating and historical for her.

I could sense her brute force and strength.

In the Bassi Pathana region of Punjab, we interviewed leader Darshan Kumar Khullar together with his mother, who sat on her *charpoy* unveiling Indian village life.

At Sharawati Prabhu's home in Mumbai, the crew enjoyed the *dosa chatni* that her mother had cooked. We filmed her parents and her workplace.

There was an immediate friendship between us, which grew even fonder during the actual expedition. She was also a Maharashtrian like me. So, it just became a special bond. We would naturally speak in Marathi, much to the envy of others, as it sounded like secret codes to them.

Sharawati, who I lovingly called 'Sharu', was already a trained mountaineer and doing her advanced course at the Nehru Institute of Mountaineering in Uttarakhand, when the principal of the school suggested her name to IMF. A gold-medallist in judo, she was physically very strong, and was also awarded the best cadet during her training in Uttarkashi.

Sharawati was also working for the Tata Group. This worked as an added advantage, as they were also sponsoring the Everest film. So, it was already a win for them to film their own employee reaching the Everest summit.

I had formed a small intimate group of friends. Sharawati, Jai

Bahuguna, Kiren Kumar, and Nandu were like my 'go-to buddies'.

Everything was planned and executed with precision. For reconnaissance, an advance party of five members—Lt Col Prem Chand, Phu Dorgee, Dorjee Lhatoo, N D Sherpa, and Dr Minoo Mehta—left Delhi for Kathmandu on 22 February.

Finally, before commencing the expedition, on a bright sunny morning on 6 March 1984, at the Parliament House, the team were called upon by the President, the Prime Minister, the Sports Minister, and the Lt Governor of Delhi, as well as Rajiv Gandhi, the Congress MP, and was given a hearty send-off with best wishes. It was during this meeting that I met the whole team and became friendly with Sharawati Prabhu, Bachendari Pal, Major Kiran Inder Kumar, Chandra Prabha Aitwal, Harshwanti Bisht, Rita Gombu, Rekha Sharma, Meena Agarwal, Magan Bissa, Sonam Palzor, Rattan Singh, and Lopsang Tshering.

The leader, Colonel Darshan Kumar Khullar, and Jai Bahuguna, who was also with me on the Antarctica expedition, were all brave and high-spirited.

The IAF plane with all the members left at 11:30 am on 7 March from Palam for Kathmandu. At the Tribhuvan International Airport, the team was received by the President of the IMF, H C Sarin, who was also the ambassador of India in Nepal.

I was always drawn to the beauty of our planet. The mountains were ready to tell a story, and the team was ready to live that story. I was ready to capture it for posterity so that millions more could be inspired by such adventurous and heroic acts.

***

Nowadays, there are advanced techniques to manage camera technologies. But in those days, we were not so lucky. The possibility for the camera to freeze was quite definite. I needed to manually winterise the camera, the opposite of tropicalised, to restrain the camera from freezing in extreme weather. It had to be customised—the eyepiece, the lens, and the inner machinery—to avoid frosting up and jamming. For extreme cases, I also carried those obsolete hand-wound spring cameras, because if nothing worked, they would.

Not only alternatives for my equipment, but the team also had to find alternatives such as using aviation fuel, known for its low freezing point, making it suitable for use in extremely cold climates.

Along with other team members, I left by road from Kathmandu to go to Jiri to start the trek and reach the base camp. The advance party established our base camp on 16 March, and a few days later, on 24 March, Camp 1 was set up at 6,050 metres.

While the team was in Jiri, Siddharth, Nandu and I decided to go back to Kathmandu to get a small aircraft for some aerial angles of the Himalayas.

We could not start the aerial filming due to erratic weather, so we decided to wait for the right time and went to sleep at the AMTREK guest house, and later went gallivanting on the streets of Kathmandu.

On my return, I received an urgent message from the base camp that our advance party had faced an avalanche near Kumbu Icefall, with a massive ice wall breaking off from Lhola.

The ice rubble and rocks had come tumbling down, overwhelming the Sherpas carrying supplies to Camp 1. In the mayhem, Sherpa Ang Rongzing was killed, and four others, seriously injured. Two of the more seriously injured sherpas were quickly evacuated by helicopter to Kathmandu for recovery, and the body of the dead sherpa was to be brought to Lukla for cremation.

We received this message on 27 March at 5.45 pm while the accident had happened on 26 March at 8.00 am. I wish I had been there to lend my hand at the evacuation and also record it.

Everest was an extraordinary experience, and despite being pitted against a team of proven expert mountaineers, we were able to keep pace with them sufficiently to shoot the film. We were experiencing conditions where avalanches occurred within a spate of moments, and where blizzard storms were everyday happenings and gave scant warning of their arrival. If I could shoot a fairly good film, I would be incredibly lucky or definitely an achiever.

***

As they say: The show must go on.

The following day, I flew over Mt Everest, shooting the Himalayas. I had previous experience of aerial shooting, pioneering the skill in India while covering the Ladakh relief operations for the I&B Ministry, and also aerial shots of the Antarctica expedition.

Aerial filming is a science and an art to adroitly capture the skies above and the scenes below. It was precariously done, as the aircraft's doors are open and you float wearing an oxygen mask and hold your camera, often in suspension.

By now, you know that I am a sucker for adventure! But I was not unprepared or unresearched.

As Siddharth and I boarded the single-engine Pilatus PC–6 Porter aircraft, I told him that 'To prepare for aerial shots at the Antarctic expedition, I had consulted experts like Bill Cartwright, the American stunt photographer who filmed the helicopter dogfights in James Bond movies like in *On Her Majesty's Secret Service.*

'Yes! Yes! I am sure you have,' Siddharth said, almost disbelieving me.

But seeing me in action, tied confidently to a monkey belt, holding the camera in mid-air, fitted with special gadgets to keep it steady and well-angled, he could not, but believe me.

My worst enemy were the vibrations coming through the gadgets. At the same time, I had to keep an eye on the right climatic conditions for filming in sub-zero temperatures.

But yes, I coped quite well, even while facing problems I had never faced before. For example, during that one instance when the aircraft had to traverse a glacial valley to get to the base of Everest and Lhotse.

Suddenly, the aircraft was hit by a downward wind, and that forced the pilot to fly towards the mountain's face. The Swiss pilot battled to bail the plane out, and by the time he regained control, he realised that we had intruded into Chinese territory.

I was literally dangling between life and death—the fear of falling through the open door into Chinese territory was one thing, and utter frustration because the film I had used had just snapped due to turbulence was another!

The aircraft personnel who had joined our team for these flights pulled me up courageously.

After regaining my breath and sanity, I looked at the broken reels, and Siddharth asked me, perplexed, 'What are we going to do now, Deepak?'

'I will have to put my hand inside the camera and join the film with tape,' I replied.

The plane circled for twenty minutes while I fixed the reel using my mastery in these techniques and a steady hand.

Those were the days when visuals could not be seen until the film was developed in the studio, unlike now, where everything is digitalised. So, we must have lost some very great shots, but I still managed to come back with some good shots.

On 31 March, the main team reached the base camp. By now Camp II was also established at 6,460 m above sea level, with Camp III being at 7,320 m above sea level.

The Everest base camp trek on the south side was at an elevation of 5,364 m (or 17,598 ft above sea level) and to date, it is one of the most popular trekking routes in the Himalayas, with about 40,000 people coming here for a trek from Lukla airport, which is at 2,846 m (or 9,337 ft above sea level) per year.

Beginning our trek to the base camp, ie., Jiri to Namche Bazar, we walked for eleven days. It was long and tiring, unlike these days, where trekkers avoid crossing huge hills and just fly to Lukla from Kathmandu.

Marching further ahead, we reached Namche Bazar, and then on 2 April, we reached Pheriche.

Hungry and tired, everyone sat down and started gorging on the food, but for me, it was suiting my taste buds.

I am very fussy as far as food goes. Sadhana knows that. God, my Sadhana, my darling Sadhana. Oh God, am I missing home at dinnertime and not when my life was at stake!

I reached the back end of the mess and prayed to the chef to help me cook what I could eat. He was kind and also knew how to cook North Indian food.

After an hour, I walked towards my tent with piping hot *dal* fry and butter *roti*.

Rajendra Sethi, deputy commissioner of police in Delhi, was trekking at Pheriche with another troop. He shared my tent and saw me coming towards it with delicious food.

He looked at me with childlike innocence and a request in his eyes, 'Can you share some of this great-smelling food?' he asked earnestly.

'Of course, I can. But for a price,' I quipped.

'You are travelling to Delhi on 10 April. My daughter is too small, and my wife is handling her all alone. Can you pay them a visit on my behalf?'

'Oh yes, I could have done that anyway but in exchange for this sumptuous meal, it is a deal.'

He was super happy to see a lovestruck man in me and to share a heavenly meal.

The temperature at Pheriche camp was 1 degree Celsius in the day, and about -5 degrees Celsius during the night.

I walked a distance of 17 km after a long seven-hour trek from Pheriche to the base camp.

And on average, we walked almost 8 km a day for twenty days from Jeri, covering spectacular terrains and dangerous altitudes, including high suspension bridges, steep inclines, and high-altitude passes.

The pristine beauty of the mountains above 16,000 ft was stunning, with a changed landscape, less oxygen, no trees, and more rocks and snow as far as the eyes could see.

***

In those days, the only means of communication were handwritten letters. The whole team wrote letters whenever the runner boys were due; these half-a-dozen boys would then run, by foot, between Kathmandu and base camps, taking and dropping the letters. We used to wait eagerly for them. These boys, along with the sherpas and local helpers, belonged to the local ethnic groups and were the backbone of our existence.

We had tragically lost one sherpa, and then there was another death—our kitchen boy, Jangbir Rai, who died of high-altitude sickness.

While having my lunch at the base camp on 15 April, I came to know that a mail runner was leaving the next day at 8 am, so I immediately thought of writing a letter for the two royalties in my life—Sadhana, and my daughter, Dhruvee, and poured my heart out.

My darling Sadhana,

How are you? I know you must be sad and missing me. But I am sure little Dhruvee must be keeping you busy enough. How is your health and all?

I have my own problems, as things are not easy for me here. Although Siddharth invited me to be on the team at the behest of Mrs Gandhi, for some unknown logic, he is not clearing me to go any higher. He may have his reasons, but he is not openly sharing them with me to work out a via media.

I am very disturbed but don't know how to go about it. I thought of getting in touch with Mrs Gandhi, but at this juncture, it doesn't seem right. I am no baby in need of mama to take care of my hurdles, right?

At the end of the day, it is just a job, so why should I

take things to heart? Just follow orders, right?

I have decided to not risk my life and stay at the basecamp instead. I will shoot whatever I can, maybe a few advertisements as planned by Siddharth.

Darling, I already feel lighter after sharing it with you. But please do not share it with anyone, not even your family. You never know when office politics take a strange angle.

In your last letter, you told me that Dhruvee has started smiling. On whom has she taken after—you or me? I hope she has your features and my talent. Your long hair and my sharp features, your homely coy style and my adventure! I am sure she is a unique blend.

We have done a great job, my dear creator.

I will soon be there to have her in my lap and you beside me.

Love you, and miss you,

Yours always,

Deepak.

I stayed back at the base camp to film the team's movement along with Nandu.

The weather was bad, but after sustained efforts, the team set up the fourth camp at 8,000 m on 29 April. The team geared up for the first attempt to climb up the mountain on 8 May, 1984.

We were told that on 9 May, Phu Dorgee, Rita Gombu, and Sherpa Ang made a summit bid at a camp setup at 8,535m, while Lt Col Prem Chand and Chandra Prabha Aitwal stayed at Camp IV.

Out of the three, Rita had to return to Camp IV as she had trouble with her oxygen gear, but Phu Dorgee and Sherpa Ang became the first two to summit without using oxygen.

This was the first time two Indian women who had reached a height of 8,000 m and above.

Sanjiv Saith was filming there as the third summit group, consisting of Bachendari Pal, Lopsang Tshering and Naib Subedar N D Sherpa went further ahead.

On 15-16 May, an avalanche hit Camp III burying six tents, and the inmates had to rip open the tent fabric with their knives to escape. Fortunately, Bachendari Pal and Lopsang Tshering had a clear escape, while Naib Subedar N D Sherpa broke his ribs, and two Nepalese guides also got injured.

Due to the avalanche, the second and third summit parties with Rekha Sharma, Latoo Dorjee, and Rattan Singh were called back to the base camp on the morning of 16 May.

At the base camp, Sharawati, Bahuguna, and I tended to them, and gave them courage to continue once the weather is better. We shared our food and the most sought-after and precious commodity—mango pickle and *kacha chivda* (flattened riceflakes) made by Sharawati's mom.

Licking her fingers, Sharu said, 'The weather seems to have improved. We can get up there tomorrow, Deepak.'

Jai interrupted, 'We shall all summit, Sharu.' I was busy wiping the pickle off my beard, and probably I ignored the comment intentionally.

On 23 May after the weather improved, a third attempt was made, which proved successful, and Bachendari Pal, Latoo Dorgee, Sonam Palzor, and Sherpa Ang Dorje reached the summit.

Bachendari Pal had set a record of being the first Indian woman mountaineer to reach the summit of Mt Everest. Four of the twenty members of the team actually scaled the peak.

Not being able to capture this grand moment through my lens became probably the only regret of my life.

But we could all hear the dispatch announcements, and Bachendari was squealing with joy. Later, we saw some amateur shots taken by the other climbers for reference.

After one team reached the peak, a terrific victory, Captain Khullar took a stand-alone decision, and the base camp was closed on 27 May, bringing the expedition to a premature halt. The team members selflessly followed the instructions, blaming their luck for coming so close, but not close enough.

Indeed, there are many slips between the cup and the lip!

The team was lifted in a Hercules helicopter that could carry 7,000 kg, and we reached Kathmandu on 2 June.

The expedition was successful, and the team was given a grand welcome at the Delhi Airport. There were media and family members, and a crowd of people waiting with flower garlands, cheering up for the team and congratulating every member who had risked their lives to create history for India.

The film was titled *Everest '84* and went on to win the best adventure film category at the 32nd National Film Awards (1985).

I threw a grand party at home, inviting all the team members. Sadhana cooked mouth-watering mutton *biryani*, and we danced and celebrated the success hoping for life to give me a second chance to get up there again, go all the way up, and photograph the mighty Himalayas.

Embracing the Digital Era

The world of cinematography evolved, and so did I. The transition from film to digital was a revolution, and I embraced it wholeheartedly. I had by now created a reservoir of visual pleasure. While purists debated its merits, I saw it as an opportunity—an era where storytelling could reach more people, where young filmmakers could create without the constraints of expensive film reels.

One day at 4:30 pm, I was planning to leave the Films Division office when my telephone rang, and I answered, 'Hello!'

It was my boss, N S Thapa!

'Haldankar, I want you to cover the President, who is attending the convocation tomorrow at 11:30 am at the Agricultural University, Pant Nagar,' he said.

'But sir, there is no direct mode of public transport reaching there at such short notice; it's not possible. Only if I go with his convoy can I make it, sir,' I replied.

'Okay, then take a chance. He hasn't left yet,' he added.

I rushed to the Rashtrapati Bhavan and called upon the press secretary, Trilochan Singh.

He was busy looking after the arrangements.

'Yes! What is it?' he asked, looking up at me.

'Sir, my team has to cover the convocation at Pant Nagar University. It would be great if we could get seats on the President's flight,' I replied.

'There are many VIPs accompanying the President on the aircraft; chances are very less, but still, you come to the technical area at 8 o' clock, and we will see,' he replied.

I came back to the office and talked to the chief sound recordist, Sita Ram, and requested him to assign a sound recordist to accompany me. He deputed K A Padmanabhan. Both of us reached the technical area sharp at 8 am.

We took a vantage position so that we could be spotted easily.

Half an hour later, the President's convoy arrived.

The President walked past the VVIPs, who had come to see them off, and climbed the staircase and boarded the aircraft.

It was a Fokker F27 Friendship, a turboprop airliner produced by the Dutch aircraft manufacturer in the Netherlands, and was also the most successful airliner of the era.

All the accompanying VVIPs boarded the aircraft.

The ladder was pulled up, and the door was about to be closed when I saw Trilochan ji standing in the doorway looking around for me.

I waved frantically; he looked in my direction and signalled me to come.

The ladder, which was in the process of being removed, was put back for me. Padmanabhan and I boarded the flight.

The President was already seated in his bulletproof glass cabin.

We had to pass through the cabin, and as we were doing so, he looked at me, eye-to-eye.

'Hello, Sir,' I greeted him with a head nod.

He immediately called out, 'Trilochan!'

'*Aeh mundey de naal gal karni haigi. Tussi enanu time allot karee!* (I have to talk with this boy. You allot him some time!)'

I swiftly looked around to see who he was talking about, and he said, '*Twadde naal gal karni hai.* (I need to speak with you.)'

I nodded, walked past and settled on a seat next to the window. Trilochan came and sat next to me curiously and inquired:

'Haldankar! What is it? Gyani *ji qui baat karna chande hai twadde nal?* (Why does Gyani *ji* wish to speak to you?)'

'I hope you don't have any grievances or representations?' He sounded curious.

'I don't have any, and I really don't know. I am just as confused as you are about why he wants to talk to me,' I replied.

It took us nearly two and a half hours to reach Pant Nagar. I kept thinking all the way about the President's strange demand.

On our return to Delhi, when we were about to land, Trilochan hurriedly came and sat next to me.

'I could help you sort out your matters with Gyani *ji*, if there are any,' he said, smiling.

We both laughed; there was a moment of awkwardness. I had none, and probably Gyani *ji* had just wanted to check who I was. By now, I was used to hearing that I had been suggested by Mrs Gandhi and even Rajiv Gandhi, who had also become a good friend. I used to film his movements too, and we used to talk for long about our mutual love i.e., of aircraft and mechanics.

I travelled tirelessly from one part of the world to the other. Covering a distance equal to one and a half times the earth's circumference along with the Prime Minister Rajiv Gandhi and President Gyani Zail Singh as they did meetings in many places and met millions, face to face.

I was now getting keen on getting a feature film to do

in Bombay, and was looking around for the right project when I was approached to make an unusually ambitious documentary that demanded extensive research, planning, and travel. I was to make a film on Manabendra Nath Roy (M N Roy), an Indian revolutionary, philosopher and radical activist. The film was to be directed by Nitish Banerjee, and scripted by Debabrata Sur Chowdhary. I had worked with Chowdhary before, and he was the subject expert for this one and had suggested my name.

M N Roy was an avid global traveller but was arrested in India and sent to jail after he returned from West Germany. He had served time in prison. We began shooting the film in India at different locations like Dehradun, Mussoorie, Almora, Kanpur, Bareilly, and Delhi. In many of these places, he had served prison terms, while he had spent the last few days of his life in Dehradun.

I captured many unknown facts about him, for example, the fact that he was invited to Russia by Lenin, and was almost his right-hand man during the Russian Revolution.

He would undertake many risky ventures on Lenin's request, including going to China for negotiations. But he had fallen out of favour with Stalin. All this was explored in the documentary, and also his extended deeds in America and Mexico. We were assigned to showcase such and many more similar but hidden facts about M N Roy.

For this one documentary, I travelled across America, Mexico, the erstwhile USSR, China, and India.

Being a documentary film, there was no character portrayal, and his life was captured through subtle images lined up in a film-like pattern.

***

East or West, home is the best.

I loved flying high to various countries, but Delhi was still my favourite.

One day, I drove my motorbike to the office, enjoying the pleasant spring of Delhi.

There was an unusual commotion in the office, and I, too, jumped into the conversation to check out what's cooking! The spirit of camaraderie was not always seen amongst my colleagues.

I heard that India was gearing up to attempt a twin approach to climb Mt Everest for the fifth time by members of the Indian Army post-monsoon, via the difficult South-West route.

God had heard my wish and given me another chance, but only if I got chosen. I think making God listen to you is easier than making humans do the same. I had apprehensions, but when had that stopped me from doing what I wished to do!

'I would want to go to Everest again, Sir,' I said assertively to my boss, N S Thapa.

To my utter surprise, he agreed readily, saying, 'Sure, Deepak, if you insist on getting up there again, why not?'

I couldn't believe my ears that I was to go with these brilliant army men with great skills, high endurance, courage, resolute determination and unequalled fortitude.

Yes, I was going to film the Indian Army film, *Mt. Everest Expedition 1985*.

Jitu Vertak vouched to come along, and I chose to take along Nanda Kumar with me, who also had experience of the Everest 1984 expedition.

The Everest Cell was established and the army men had already begun endurance training in the past few weeks, doing activities like freestyle rock climbing on the natural Aravalli rock face with the Indian Mountaineering Federation (IMF).

The procurement of necessary equipment, tables for travel, clothing, tentage, and rations was in full swing.

I felt very humbled and delighted when, as part of their training, they were shown my earlier film on Indian Women on Everest 1984 in January 1985. The film was screened at the prestigious Vigyan Bhavan, a location where important government meetings in New Delhi, regularly take place. For the final selection, the team was milling around in the Garhwal Himalayan region, supported by the Nehru Institute of Mountaineering (IMF) located in Uttarkashi.

This training in Feb-April was crucial. They practised climbing Mt Everest by considering climbing the great Mt Shivling, a dramatic peak, visually very striking, and looking like a giant granite tooth clad with ice and difficult to climb, making it a famed achievement for mountaineers.

I was not a part of this training programme; nonetheless, I decided to take part in the endurance building in Dharamshala and reached Pathankot at 4:30 am on 6 June 1985, and eventually Dharmshala at 7:30 pm.

We were put up in tents, but as luck would have it, it started raining very heavily, making our tents tear up and fly away like paper. Somehow, we managed to get by during that night.

But Col Prem Chand woke me up at 5:30 am.

'Deepak, come on, wake up! Let's go; it's time for the training,' he said.

At McLeod Ganj, he made me climb a wall with a harness tied around my waist.

The young boy in me felt exhilarated as I felt I was getting trained to be a 'gentleman cadet' of the Indian Military!

I was also made to trek for hours with loads of 20 kg over the undulating terrain of the Himachal hills to build up endurance.

On 13 June, at 7 am, I walked for two hours to reach a place called Triund, a popular McLeod Ganj trekking site, at a height of 9,000 feet.

Three days later, on 16 June, I got back to Dharamshala, safe and sound. Here we were blessed by the Dalai Lama, who also presented a small statue of Lord Buddha to be placed at the summit of Qomolongma, facing Tibet (Mount Everest is known locally as Qomolongma).

'What will be the fate of our team?' I asked the Dalai Lama.

'If and when the blessed Mother Qomolongma calls, only then will you go!' he said with a hearty laugh.

To my delight and surprise, a medical advice was issued to increase our beer and rice consumption for a couple of days. The idea was to put on weight while in the hinterlands and shed all that weight when up in the mountains.

I got the logic at once! And who questions such sanctions?

The team returned via Udhampur and also visited Vaishnodevi. This climb was an expedition in itself with its narrow, jagged, hairpin winding pathways. We had to walk through dark cavernous tunnels with icy waters flowing ankle-deep.

Successfully completing the strenuous training, meeting the Dalai Lama, and visiting Vaishnodevi had raised the positive energy and fervour as we reached Delhi on 27 June 1985.

Ready to depart on 21 July, an advance party comprising Major K V Cherian, Captain D B Thapa, Havildar Neema Sherpa and N K Jaswant Singh boarded an AN-32 IAF aircraft for Kathmandu, Nepal. They moved in a sortie of two AN-32 aircraft with 1,500 loads, each of 20 kg (Sherpa) load, for further ascent on the mountain.

At Kathmandu, Captain D B Thapa and Havildar Neema Sherpa were received by representatives of Yeti Travels, the agency in charge of providing competent sherpas to our team.

Major K V Cherian and N K Jaswant Singh went about establishing liaison and communications. At the embassy, they received Rs 3 lakh as advance payment for Sonam Girmi, the Sherpa *sardar* who had come down from the mountains to meet them in Kathmandu and take them up via Namche Bazar to the base camp.

The loads were to be moved through the jungles and ravines from Jiri, first by yaks and then by sherpas.

As these three people who had gone ahead completed the preparations, the last leg of the preparation now remained to be done. And we had to also call upon and report to the dignitaries as part of the official protocol.

The team reached the President's house in the yellow room —the yellow drawing room at the Rashtrapati Bhavan, the official residence of the President of India, is used for smaller state functions. Here we were supposed to meet the Prime Minister, the Vice President, the Defence Minister, the Sports Minister, and the Chief of Army Staff.

Tragically, the leader, Lt Col Prem Chand, had met with an accident on 22 July 1985 with a DTC bus, breaking his left carpal bones, and sadly, he met us all with his arm in a plaster.

Anyway, the leader, Lt Col Prem Chand, the deputy leader, the Chief of Army, General A S Vaidya, and many other high-ranking officers and I were waiting enthusiastically for the introductions with the President, Gyani *Ji*.

After an introduction and handshake with the leaders and others, the President approached me. With a strong, firm handshake, I introduced myself.

'Sir, I am Deepak Haldankar, newsreel officer, Films Division.' While he was still shaking hands with me, I could see a sparkle in his eyes, an indication of recognition. Still holding my hand, he looked around and called out, 'Trilochan! *Tussi e munde de nal gal karne da* time *allot ni kitta si*? (Trilochan, you did not arrange a time to meet this boy.)'

Trilochan was perplexed and did not know what to say. There was silence all around.

Just then, I broke the silence and said, 'Sir, I am leaving for the expedition to Everest and will return in three months. Can we talk after I come?'

Trilochan plunged in and said, '*Odde baad date lagata hun ji* (I will fix his appointment after that, Sir.'

Gyani *ji* nodded, smiled and said: '*Oh haan, zaroor odde baad milaange. Koi gal ni.* (No problem, we will definitely meet after that.)'

Standing beside me was Major Vijay Sharma, who had lost two fingers of his right arm due to frostbite and exposure to severe cold in an earlier expedition.

Gyani *ji* looked at General Vaidya with anguish, who explained that all medical expenses were paid, and he was also given a bravery medal.

Hearing this he said, '*Bas itna hi?* (Is that all?)'

He then whispered something to Trilochan, who made a note in his diary. After the introductions got over, he came and handed over a cheque of Rs 25,000 to Major Vijay, which used to be a big amount in those days.

Everyone in the room congratulated Major Vijay as it felt good to be acknowledged for the sacrifices one makes for the nation.

On 4 August, after a last round of loading of the equipment, the team, led by Lt Col Prem Chand, boarded an AN-12 aircraft of the Indian Air Force from the Palam Airfield, New Delhi, and landed at Kathmandu Airport. Here we were all received by his excellency, H C Sarin, and staff.

Bikram Pandey, the co-ordinator from Yeti Travel Agency, greeted us with marigold garlands and scarves. Earlier, he had received the advance party of Major K C Cherian.

We were lodged in a four-star hotel, the Shangri-La, in Kathmandu. It was a very comfortable stay, and I missed having Sadhana and Dhruvee by my side.

I sat down to write a letter to Sadhana before embarking on the ascent. Funnily, the ballpoint pen was almost frozen because of the cold, and I had to warm it with our age-old technique of licking and rubbing it often.

I couldn't write much, but did suggest that, if possible, they could come to receive me at Kathmandu on my way back, explaining the economics of it, as in, 'The ticket to Kathmandu is about a thousand rupees one-way, and from Kathmandu Airport to Hotel Shangri-La is about 50 rupees; maybe you could come to receive me on my return.'

I wasn't sure if she would agree, with a baby in hand. But since childhood, I had fulfilled all my wishes only by driving them hard. So maybe if I drove this desire hard enough, I might get to see my family much before I reached Delhi.

On 8 August, the team visited Pattan, a whole village built solely on logs of wood!

It was a very pleasing sight. I had about Rs 4,000 on me, and while the others were busy buying Dictaphones, stereocassette players, batteries, etc., I wanted to buy a Philips music system, which I had seen for Rs 3,900. It was either that or other sundry things like a hand-operated sewing machine, one toy frog with a watch dial and music, one ballpoint pen with a watch, or one solar calculator. I even managed to get myself two safari suits stitched with local cloth!

The team left Hotel Shangri-La by the evening, drove to the embassy, attended *puja* there and departed for Jiri in a bus. The bus reached Jiri at midnight, after covering a distance of 120 km on 11 August, and the next day, about 8.00 am in the morning, we left Jiri.

The very first day, we trekked from Jiri to Shivalaya, a beautiful tourist destination with an old temple of Shiv *ji* and to Changama, then finally to Bhandar.

On the way from Sete to Namtola, the trek became very pleasant and memorable for me and Jitu.

Jitu Vartak, Lt Bakshi, and I stopped at a bathing point and enjoyed a crisp cold bath in the open.

The team departed early from Numtola on 16 August. Crossing the river here was tough and dramatic, as the loads and men were pulled across the river, one by one. I wanted to film these brave men, but to do that, I had to negotiate the rope bridge and trek steep heights. Happily, I put my training to use and conducted some daring and action-packed photography.

I was quite satisfied with my shots.

We finally reached Namche Bazar on 19 August and were housed at a lodge called International Trekkers Foot Lodge.

On 21 August, the leader of the expedition had to be replaced by Brigadier Jagjit Singh, as Lieutenant Colonel Prem Chand was advised to look after his health. He arrived in a helicopter, and we all assembled to receive him. He brought mail along with him, and I received letters from Papa and Sadhana.

We had walked 160 km from 9 August from Jiri to Namche Bazar, which was the last stop with electric lights.

The following day, we marched from Namche Bazar and on 28 August at 4:30 pm, reached the Everest basecamp.

The scenic beauty on the way through Periche, Lobuche, and Gorakshep was too good to be true, as if it was Heaven on Earth.

We all stopped at Gorakshep to acclimatise, having passed through Khumbu and its dehydrating moraines. On the way, we came across memorials of the deceased mountaineers on Everest, including Major Harsh Bahuguna, the elder brother of Major Jai Bahuguna.

I was not leaving any chance of filming raw and unfiltered moments and the beauty of the mountains.

At 1,900 feet, I shot and captured the footage of the army men inhaling oxygen, their deep struggles and gasps of air alongside the vast beauty of the surrounding Himalayas.

The weather was not very favourable. It would snow every day, and the temperature would dip down to -10 degrees Celsius.

These were the real 'Soldiers on Everest,' I told Colonel Ashok Pratap Tanwar and Captain Prem Prakash.

'Mountaineering is the most hazardous sport,' I said, and they agreed.

It was exhilarating to film these members, and I would run around the mountains and small walking paths with my camera chasing those wonderful army men, dealing with my camera batteries and all, capturing the moments without disrupting their routine or putting any of us at risk. There was zero margin of error, as a single mistake would cost me my life. I wanted my audience through my film to understand how much hard work this was and how much everyone suffered during the process.

In my earlier documentaries, I had enough ground to place myself at a stable spot like a *shikari* (hunter), pointing my camera to take that one brilliant shot, and here, ideally, I wanted to position myself up on the top of the famous Hilary Step and record the climber scaling the iconic cliff, on the top of the world. I continued with the team, climbing and struggling to move forward along with my film camera, tripod, still cameras, all my batteries and my oxygen cylinder.

Probably the sherpas and I were carrying similar weight, but that did not deter me from capturing the surreal beauty of the place, consuming the sheer crispness of the air, the white tranquillity of the surroundings, and the eerie howling of the winds racing across the mountains.

On 5 September 1985, we reached Kumbo Glacier.

***

It was the end of September, and a month had passed on the mountains. The very final list of mountaineers was getting finalised. All in the team wanted to receive the national flag to be hoisted at Mt Everest.

It was decided to make two-pronged attempts, one facing South-West, led by Major Jai Bahuguna, and the standard South Col and South-East Ridge route, led by Major Kiran Inder Kumar.

It was very shocking and disheartening when we heard that Major Inder Kumar had met a deadly fate when he decided to move ahead despite extremely bad weather. The temperatures dropped to -17 degrees Celsius at basecamp, and -45 degrees Celsius at Mt Everest; it was impossible to move. I decided to not move further ahead of Camp II or death was inevitable.

He had radioed at 3.00 pm, saying that his oxygen mask was leaking and that Bakshi had lost his goggles.

Half an hour later, Bakshi, unclear about what had happened, reported that Inder Kumar was gone. He apparently fell from 8,500 metres, and his broken body was found at the foot of the Lhotse fence in the western CWM two hours later.

I felt very painful recording this event on my film. The whole team was sorrowful. Major Jai Bahuguna requested by radio to be relieved of his leadership on the South-West face, and he joined the South Col party to spend the night in anguish, along with five others. Inder Kumar was a very experienced mountaineer, so there was no question about his decision, but it broke everybody's heart and spirit.

The expedition must go on.

Bahuguna had kept two of his men, Captain Vijay Pal Singh Negi, and Lieutenant M U Bhaskar Rao, with him. Bakshi and Havildar Rigzin Namgyal and L K Negi also chose to stay behind, as they were exhausted and badly frostbitten. The weather continued to be excruciating.

But on the morning of 9 October, Namgyal and L K Negi decided to descend, but could not do so as they could not locate their ropes in the snow. The next morning, the same thing happened with worsening weather.

Jai Bahuguna radioed to share the predicament, followed by an urgent call from Rao. Immediately a rescue party was sent, but they had to return halfway up the Lhotse Face.

The next day, Captain Prem Prakash, Havildar I B Gurung and two Sherpas set out to rescue them and reached South Col at 4 pm.

They found Bakshi and Negi dead under a collapsed tent, and Bahuguna and Rao both barely alive outside another tent. Resuscitation was tried, but they too, took their last breaths.

The loss of these five brave army men was a massive setback for the expedition. We felt broken, our spirits torn to pieces. The news of the disaster had started doing the rounds through the grapevine surely all the way to Kathmandu, if not Delhi.

The leader had to take a quick call, and he decided on new plans for the expedition.

On 26 October, we made our fifth summit attempt. Accompanying them voluntarily were Captain Banerjee and Jitu Vartak.

I, along with Captain Tanwar, moved to Gorakshep and then to Kala Patthar for the final film photo cover of the summit attempt. Nathang and six porters moved to Lobuche to bring up the remaining rations as a last move up.

The snow and slush and our demoralised souls were making movement difficult.

We needed a boost, any boost, when we got a surprise message at Kala Patthar from the twin huts of the green Gorakshep.

'Deepak, the American President is nearby,' Captain Tanwar mentioned to me eagerly.

'Yeah, Kala Patthar is the ideal place for anyone who wants to have a close but safe look at Everest,' I replied.

We received an invitation from President Jimmy Carter to join him and his troops at Kala Patthar.

They expressed their condolences at our huge loss, and offered refreshments and soft drinks as we viewed the peaks together. The president also shared how proud he was that we had decided to complete the mission, nonetheless.

'Wishing all of you the best for scaling the peak,' he said, showing us a thumbs up.

The last determined effort, our sixth attempt, was also unsuccessful as well, and we now had to move down and wind up the entire crew at the base camp.

Barring that small event of meeting the American President, we were all very sad and lifeless inside. The descent felt like an albatross on our weary shoulders.

Witnessing and filming such tragedy was excruciating, but I allowed myself to really live in the moment. I packed my belongings from the Everest basecamp, where today often dozens freeze and turn back, thinking I did have a story to tell through my lens.

I let my inner *Dronacharya* ask me, 'What do you see in front?' And I mentally replied, 'The bird's eye!' My bird's-eye stories were as many as I could capture—good, bad and ugly!

A photograph freezes a moment; cinematography teaches it how to breathe.

Chaya Devi Haldankar with her husband, Raghunath Sambhaji Haldankar (left); Chaya Devi Haldankar holding her infant son, Deepak Haldankar (4 months old), Dharwar Hospital, 17 December 1948).

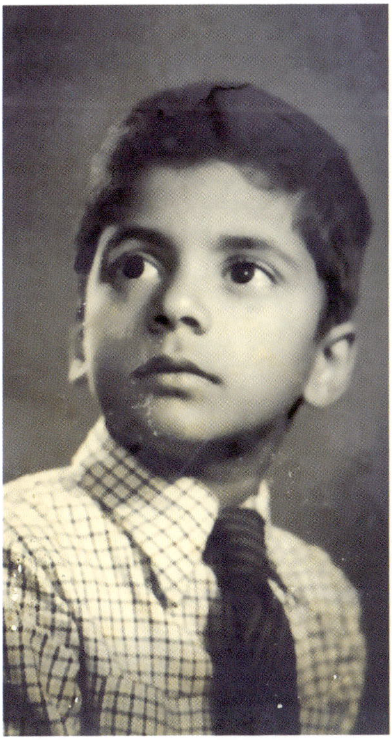

Deepak Haldankar as a young child, dressed for St Xavier's Church School, Belgaum.

Deepak Haldankar with his grandfather, parents, younger brother, Kiran Haldankar, and the family pet, Kalu.

Deepak Haldankar with his parents and younger brother, Kiran Haldankar, Belgaum, 1953.

A City of Sleepless Dreams

Deepak Haldankar with his parents and brothers, Kiran and Anand Haldankar (left); Making way for his passion: Deepak Haldankar's early days in still photography.

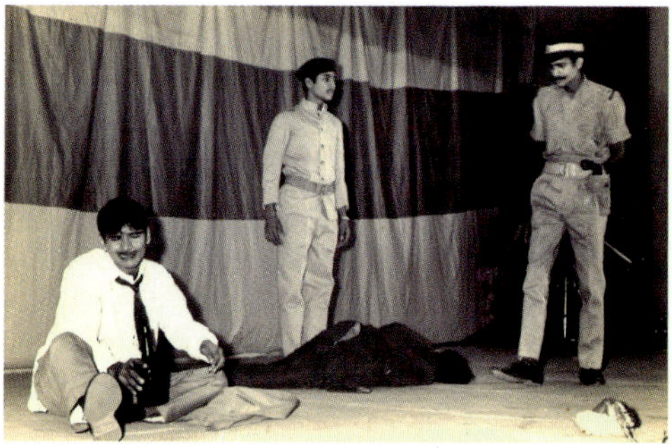

Papa's gems: Kiran, Anand, and Deepak Haldankar (left); Performing on stage in the play "Five Minutes to Satan" at Chennai College, 1966.

Close-up portrait of Deepak Haldankar at Chennai College, October 1968 (left); Winner of the elocution competition sponsored by Holy Family High School, 1965 (middle); Filming at Sundarwadi, Malad, Mumbai, November 1970 (right).

The Third Eye—My Camera Lens

Deepak Haldankar filming the prestigious 15 August celebrations, taking a stance like a lion (left); Deepak Haldankar with a robust 35mm film movie camera, featuring a prominent film magazine—a tool of classic cinema.

Outside the Films Division office, 10 Pandara Road, in New Delhi with colleagues. (left); Deepak Haldankar with the Arriflex 16ST, a classic 16mm motion picture camera.

Deepak Haldankar filming Sanjay Gandhi (left); Practising shooting on Juhu Beach.

This is how Deepak Haldankar walked in for the UPSC examination (left); Deepak Haldankar proudly displaying his love for firearms (middle); Proudly flaunting his camera and film magazine (right).

Deepak Haldankar with his first Rolleicord camera (left); Holding a professional-grade film camera, featuring a coiled cable connected to an external power source and recording equipment (middle); Deepak Haldankar with his first Vitessa camera—a 35mm compact rangefinder (right).

Deepak Haldankar discussing a shot with Milkha Singh while filming *The Flying Sikh*. (left); Inside the stadium, Deepak Haldankar filming the legend as he runs like the wind.

Bittersweet Memories

Deepak Haldankar with Ila Arun (left); Rama Pandey clicked by Deepak Haldankar.

Deepak Haldankar filming the Bastar tribe in action.

Deepak Haldankar carrying an Arriflex camera on a monopod (left); Filming in Bastar, wearing a *langot* (middle); Deepak Haldankar with Tripti Pandey and Ila Arun during the filming of *Mundan* (right).

A Love Story in the Sky

A blooming romance—holding hands at Lodhi Gardens (left); Deepak Haldankar and Sadhana Haldankar at Lodhi Gardens, Delhi.

Sadhana Haldankar, solo in a sari.

Sadhana and Deepak Haldankar celebrating their 40th wedding anniversary.

A simple wedding ceremony with close friends and colleagues.

Rubbing Shoulders with the World's Best

French explorer and author Michael Peissel with Sadhana Haldankar (left); Deepak Haldankar with Michael Peissel from France with his hovercraft team; Major D N Das is on the extreme left.

Filming during Prince Charles' wedding procession through the streets of the UK (left); Prince Charles' wedding, United Kingdom.

Deepak Haldankar with Italian filmmaker, Michelangelo Antonioni (left); Deepak Haldankar on London Bridge.

Deepak Haldankar preparing for a hovercraft ride—Expedition Ganga.

Expedition Ganga '82—Deepak Haldankar on the raft, ready to shoot. (*An expedition similar in spirit to Edmund Hillary's 'Ocean to Sky.'*)

Deepak Haldankar filming the ASC (Army Service Corps) moments before the grand fall.

Conquering the Frozen Frontier

Filming Mrs Indira Gandhi for A Day with the Prime Minister (left); Filming Mrs Indira Gandhi addressing a rally in Orissa.

Second Indian Antarctic Expedition team with Mrs Indira Gandhi at the centre; Dr S Z Qasim (leader of the first expedition) is on her right; V K Raina is on her left and Shivraj Patil (then Science & Technology Minister) is on the far right.

Deepak Haldankar travelling with Mrs Indira Gandhi (left); Deepak Haldankar—a man, a camera, and the Antarctic wilderness.

Deepak Haldankar on deck just before the iceberg disappeared (left); Deepak Haldankar in conversation with an aircraft fuel engineer, camera in hand.

Deepak Haldankar changing film inside a black bag (left); Deepak Haldankar filming scientists from the ship's bridge.

Deepak Haldankar travelling with 21 suitcases—his preferred way (left); The Second Indian Scientific Expedition aboard the Polar Circle, ready to embark.

A Legacy in Frames

Deepak Haldankar with Meera Dewan during the shoot of *Gift of Love* (left); Hercules Aircraft airlifting the team back home.

Indian Everest '84 team members meeting Buta Singh.

Indian Everest '84 team members with Rajiv Gandhi (left); With Sharawati Prabhu in Gurugram.

Deepak Haldankar with Gyani Zail Singh and Siddharth Kak (left); Deepak Haldankar in Kathmandu for aerial filming of Everest.

Embracing the Digital Era

Deepak Haldankar with Nitish Banerjee and Debarata Sur Chowdhury during the shoot of a film on M N Roy (left); Deepak Haldankar with Jitu Vartak and Nandh Kumar, ready for the grand climb.

Deepak Haldankar trekking toward Mount Everest from Sete–Namtola (left); Deepak Haldankar meeting the Himalayan tribe en route to Everest.

Deepak Haldankar receiving blessings from His Holiness the Dalai Lama.

Filming the Himalayas and Everest peak from the helicopter *CHETAK* (left); Everest Base Camp, 1985.

Deepak Haldankar with his Arriflex camera at Everest Base Camp, 1985.

Deepak Haldankar with the U S President Jimmy Carter at Kala Patthar (left); Deepak Haldankar ready to fly in *CHETAK*, gazing at Everest with joy (middle); Deepak Haldankar inside the AN-32 Hercules aircraft (right).

Reflections on Life and Death Through the Lens

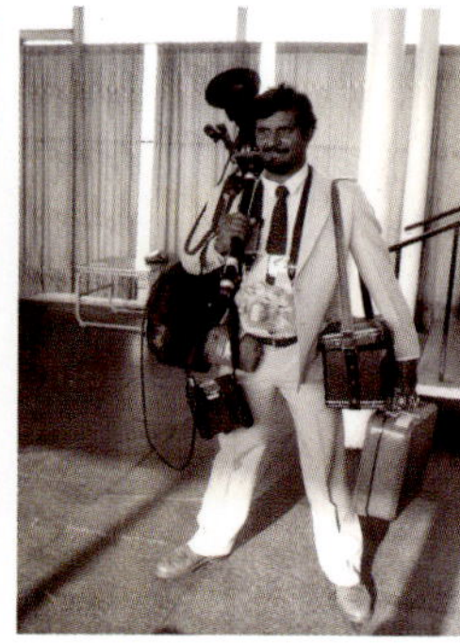

Deepak Haldankar with the Aaton XTR Prod 16mm camera, often called the 'Cat on your shoulder' (left); In conversation with Begum Abida Ahmed (middle); Deepak Haldankar at Moscow Airport, 16 July 1989. A one-man army—this was his usual way to travel (right).

Deepak Haldankar in China during a four-day state visit with Rajiv Gandhi.

With Sheikh Mujibur Rahman, Dhaka, 19 June early 1970s (left); Filming the 26th January Parade—his set position every year to capture the Prime Minister hoisting the national flag.

With B D Jatti, former Vice President of India, and his wife, Shrimati Sangamma, on the Tanzania tour (left); With former Palestinian National Authority President, Yasser Arafat.

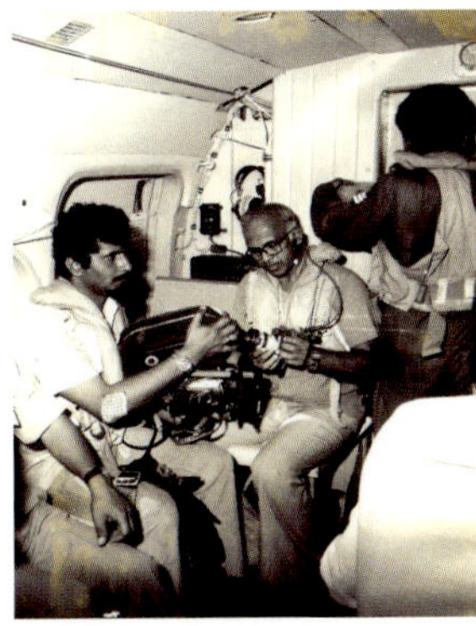

Walking the red carpet to another chartered flight (left); Exhausted inside a chartered aircraft, holding his favourite gun.

With Vice President B D Jatti in his chamber, New Delhi, before proceeding to East Africa.

Filming Tito's funeral, recording the grief and loss through the camera's eyepiece.

On tour with Rajiv Gandhi, meeting Lalith Athulathmudali during India–Sri Lanka diplomatic engagement.

Travelling with the delegation inside former Prime Minister Narasimha Rao's chartered plane.

With former President Fakhruddin Ali Ahmed and Begum Abida Ahmed at their Delhi residence; Deepak Haldankar received a special award for this documentary.

Be-Mulk Nawab

Deepak Haldankar with Baby Dhruvee.

Dhruvee with Daddy's camera.

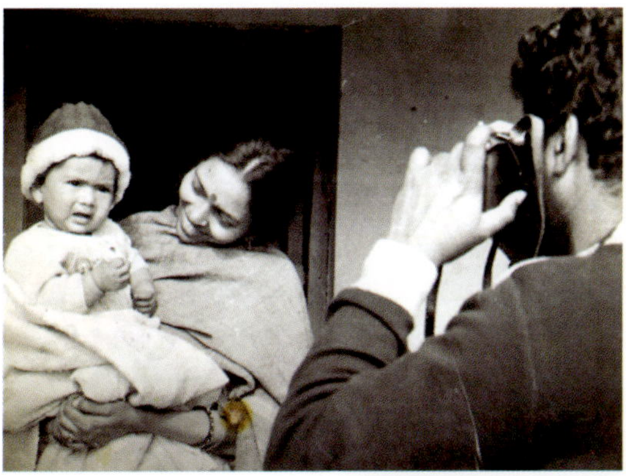

Deepak Haldankar photographing Sadhana and Dhruvee.

Dhruvee, heroine in the making—photographed by Daddy.

Dhruvee in white—headshot.

Dhruvee solo

Dhruvee—headshot by Deepak Haldankar.

Dhruvee solo

The Last Shot, A New Beginning

Deepak Haldankar selecting a frame for his shot.

Deepak Haldankar with Padma Khanna during *Champaran Ke Gaon.*

Deepak Haldankar with Health Minister B Shankaranand, 1984 (left); Deepak Haldankar with former Indian Minister of Communications, Ram Vilas Paswan.

Deepak Haldankar with Tarsem Antil (left); Looking through a Red One camera.

In-action shooting for an advertisement produced by Filmsmiths.

While shooting the documentary *Bonds of Bagpath* on Revolver Dadis—Chandra Tomar, and Prakashi Tomar (left); Deepak Haldankar—beauty lies in the eyes of the beholder.

Reflections on Life and Death Through the Lens

As my career expanded, so did my understanding of life. Cinematography had given me everything—adventure, love, recognition—but it also demanded sacrifice. The long hours, the sleepless nights, the time away from family.

I returned from the Everest expedition and found that Sadhana was busy hosting Bimba. Whenever Gyani *ji* visited Bangalore, he would make it a point to spend time at Bimba's house with his delegation. Bimba Raikar was affluent. She was my cousin, Daulat *Dada*'s elder sister, and was also a Member of Parliament.

I remember one day in Delhi, Bimba was on the phone, speaking to Trilochan Singh, and reminding him to confirm her meeting with Gyani *ji,* when Sadhana just casually mentioned, 'Bimba *ji,* Dhruvee and I have not seen the Rashtrapati Bhavan, can we come with you too?'

Covering the telephone mouthpiece with her hands, she confirmed, nodding her head. 'I am bringing guests with me to the Parliament, Mr Trilochan,' she added.

Bimba, along with Sadhana and little Dhruvee, was shown to the President's office. He received Bimba very warmly, and requested her to take a seat across his table.

After their discussion, he enquired, 'Bimba, where are you staying in Delhi?'

'At my brother's place; this is my *Bhabhi* and their daughter,' she replied.

'You have a brother living in Delhi?' he asked, surprised.

'Yes, I do, and he is a newsreel officer. His name is Deepak Haldankar,' she mentioned.

He tried to recollect where he had heard the name.

'I tried a few times to meet Deepak! He is a very busy man,' he said.

Sadhana later narrated what had happened.

There was a pause at that moment; Bimba was a little taken aback, not realising what was coming next. It was a 'life applauding' moment for me!

Bimba asked Gyaniji, inquisitively, 'What happened, is everything okay?'

His speech was punctuated with bursts of applause. 'I wanted to put forward his name to award him with a Padma Shree!'

Sadhana stood by me like a rock. Actually, no, a rock is hard. She stood by my side like a strong shrub of *parijaat* (night jasmine)—dependable, perennial, and sweet as hell! I am eternally grateful to her.

When Pope John Paul II visited India in 1986, I was called to cover his tour.

It was an honour to film Pope John Paul's visit to India on my ARRIFLEX 16 SR (16mm) camera, as he went about meeting Indian dignitaries, like Prime Minister Rajiv Gandhi, President Zail Singh, and others.

Being an avid admirer of Gandhi *ji,* he visited Rajghat, and called him a hero of humanity and a harbinger of love.

He also met Mother Teresa to acknowledge her tireless and selfless services. He met with some Indian tribal communities like Khasis and Garos, spreading the message of love, pride and culture. He also spent a day in Chennai, meeting many religious leaders. He also visited Goa, and called upon the Catholics to preserve and promote the moral and religious values of Christianity. He then went to Kerala to beatify Sr Alphonso and Fr Kuriakose Elias Chavarra.

He concluded his visit at Delhi at a religious cultural event hosted at the Indira Gandhi Stadium, saluting the nation and its people.

His visit touched my heart as well as the hearts of millions of Indians because when he stepped on Indian soil, he kissed the Indian soil, and as he was leaving, he quoted Tagore:

Where the mind is without fear and the head is held high,
Where knowledge is free…
Into that heaven of freedom, my father, let my country awake.

Meeting him and filming him, my conviction grew stronger that 'the first test of a truly great man is his humility.'

The film was titled *The Pope Meets India* and at the 34th National Film Festival, 1987, it won a national award for the best news film.

***

In the summer month of June, Delhi's temperature can go up to 45 degrees Celsius, and the best time to get out of the house is either early morning or late in the evening.

A popular tourist destination, India Gate in Delhi was open twenty-four hours a day, where people came to pay their respects to the martyred soldiers at Amar Jawan Jyoti and to meander around on the green grass, playing with their kids, families, or partners, and eating *bhelpuri* (a tangy, savoury snack) or ice-cream. It was my regular route to reach my office.

One day, I had taken my brother-in-law, Nitin Mathur, a.k,a. Babloo, as my pillion rider. The place was full of life and commotion as men, women, and children were enjoying a cool evening after the blistering afternoon.

I was driving leisurely around when Babloo suddenly screamed, 'Jija *ji*, look, Rajiv Gandhi and Sonia Gandhi.'

I turned around and saw them driving casually by in an open jeep!

'Hey Derek Haldee!' Rajiv Gandhi yelled and waved at me.

Sonia Gandhi smiled and asked, 'Is he the adventure filmmaker?'

'Yes! He is the adventure filmmaker Derek Haldee!' Rajiv replied.

Rajiv Gandhi would often call me Derek after the American actor and photographer John Derek, who was also known for launching the career of his fourth wife, Bo Derek.

I loved him calling me 'Derek Haldee' as it felt like something straight out of a James Bond movie.

Just like Indira Gandhi, Rajiv Gandhi was also very fond of me.

The next morning, I received a letter from Rajiv Gandhi. It was about him wanting to know about the Antarctica Expedition since I had gone as a one-man army to Antarctica without any assistants.

He wanted to know from me, firsthand, about my personal experiences, difficulties and suggestions for the planning of future expeditions.

Rajiv Gandhi had taken office after the assassination of his mother, Indira Gandhi.

At the age of 40, he had become the youngest Indian Prime Minister. He was also a trained pilot, and a member of the flying club.

I met Rajiv Gandhi in the days that followed and told him how honoured I felt to share my assessment of the second scientific expedition to Antarctica.

'The expedition was the most successful one, in the sense that it fulfilled all the objectives and aims it set out to meet,' I asserted.

'I feel the expedition succeeded in selecting permanent sites and laying the base and logistics for future expeditions,' I continued.

'What were your difficulties, Derek? And please tell me if you have any suggestions,' he asked with concern.

I grew bold with his warmth and said, 'I would like to suggest, sir, that greater attention be paid to the role of the media in future expeditions. It appeared to me that there was not sufficient understanding of the need for and importance of the media in the expedition.'

I was on a roll, and spoke my heart out: 'We must recognise that it is the media only that brings these happenings, achievements and accomplishments of such accomplished and epoch-making expeditions before the world at large. Inclusion of more media personnel and a higher priority rating in the scheme of things would, I feel, be a better thing. After all, *jungle mein mor nacha, kisi ne na dekha*! (A peacock may dance all he pleases in the jungle, but if no one saw it, it didn't dance as such!), right sir?' I asked.

'Hmmm...' he was listening with full concentration.

I was happy with the ear he was giving me and went on to share a heroic deed I had done.

'Sir, for the record, I would also like to share an incident which may interest you,' I said.

'Please tell me, I would like to know,' he asked inquisitively.

'I saved the expedition from a disaster, Sir. By mistake, the attendant filled the fuel meant for the snow scooters into the helicopter tank.'

'What!' he was shocked. Being a pilot, he knew the dire implications of such an act.

'Sir, you know from our earlier conversations that I like to observe mechanical details. I saw this mechanical error and brought it to the fueler's attention. The whole tank was then rinsed and refilled with the right fuel,' I concluded.

'Wow, what a save, Derek! I have made note of your great act of composure and quick-thinking!' he said with appreciation.

I accompanied Rajiv Gandhi on many of his foreign tours in the next few years, like the trip to Bhutan in September 1985, when he went to strengthen Indo-Bhutan relations, and in October 1985, when he went to the Bahamas to build Indo-Bahamas relations.

Rajiv Gandhi would come across as a very suavé, young, friendly gentleman with a smile to die for, and walking by his side was much more than just a matter of pride.

Around him, I made sure that I was always aptly dressed in shiny shoes, and, with pride I would have a still camera PRAKTICA SUPER TL 1000 slung around my neck, and a film camera on my shoulder.

Those days, the PRAKTICA SUPER TL 1000 I used, was a 35 mm camera with a single-lens reflex. It was a good camera, but I had to manually fix the right focus on this equipment because its manufacturer, VEB Pentacon, who had produced the camera in 1980–84, did not build auto-focus, and therefore I had to focus by hand.

The camera had a built-in light meter, and the exposure meter was designed to measure exposure through the lens of the camera. I would select the aperture and shutter speed manually and use an external flash connected via a hot shoe.

With my PRAKTICA SUPER TL 1000, I often used the 50 mm 2.8 Carlzeiss Jena Tessar lens, famous amongst big photographers. It was called 'Adlerauge' in German, which means 'Eagle's eye' because it was considered super sharp.

Technology was rapidly changing, and so was my choice of cameras.

I remember my initial entry camera, ROLLEICORD, founded by a German manufacturer of optical instruments in 1920, which I was so fond of.

Papa had also bought me an ANSCOFLEX II A camera, created in 1954 by Ansco, but designed by a very impressive industrial designer named Raymond Loewy, popularly known as the designer of the Shell gas station logo. This camera had a metal body, and a raised matting around the lenses, with a rugged rubber-like strap that was built into the camera body. The front lens cover was made of aluminium slides to reveal both lenses, as well as act as a glare blocker from the viewfinder—I loved this unique design.

Another of my favourite cameras was the EXAKTA VAREX PENTAX; it was produced in various variations due to copyright issues of the Varex brand by lhagee in Dresden from 1950–1970.

Mine was based on the previous model, the Kine Exakta, the

first commercially produced 35mm single-lens reflex camera.

It was truly a masterpiece; I owned it and used it frequently.

Rajiv Gandhi had married the Italian Sonia, and she accompanied her husband on his political tours. He would attend events with his delegation, and Sonia would, on the same tour, have a separate programme. They travelled to Syria to meet Prime Minister Zoubi and Mrs Zoubi, visited Umayyad Mosque, and also met President Assad; they travelled to the Federal Republic of Germany, and addressed the special function jointly hosted by the Federation of German Industries, the German Association of Industry and Trade, and the German Foreign Policy Associations.

Sonia Gandhi also accompanied Rajiv Gandhi when he addressed the third special session of the UN General Assembly devoted to disarmament. They also travelled together to Hungary for the wreath-laying ceremony at Heroes Square, meeting Prime Minister Grosz, representatives of the Indo-Hungarian Friendship Circle, and Hungarian Indologists.

I was to travel with them to Jordan, Spain, Yugoslavia, Belgrade, and Turkey. The film crew would, before every trip, receive a little white book with the emblem *Satyamev Jayate* embossed on it. It would have the Prime Minister's printed itinerary, and a detailed guide for him and his entourage to get acquainted with the local weather conditions and other miscellaneous information.

I shadowed the Prime Minister's movement everywhere he went, with my film and still camera and all my other filming paraphernalia like lights, batteries, extra boxes of Kodak 35 mm film, and the almost extinct ILFORD PAN 400 black and white film that was my personal favourite.

Most of their photos from that era are my captures.

Jumping from one chartered flight to another, walking on one red carpet to another, I literally rubbed shoulders with VVIPs and dignitaries and lived a life many would desire.

I remember a very funny incident when I was accompanying Mrs Indira Gandhi on her tour to Yugoslavia for President Josip Broz Tito's funeral in Dedinje, Belgrade, Serbia. Tito was very popular and was viewed as the central unifying figure of the culturally and religiously diverse and ethnically antagonistic nation of Yugoslavia.

At the funeral, there were a significant number of statesmen from Western, Eastern and Non-Aligned countries across the world, including four kings, six princes, twenty-two prime ministers, thirty-one presidents, and forty-seven ministers of foreign affairs. In total, one hundred and twenty-eight countries out of the one hundred and fifty-four UN members at the time were represented, along with delegates from seven multilateral organisations, six movements and forty political parties. Needless to say, there were so many media personnel from all over the world.

I was following Mrs Gandhi. And apart from the usual film camera on one shoulder and the PRAKTICA still camera on the other shoulder, I had an extra gadget with me—a big foldable aluminium six-step ladder around my neck!

Mrs Indira Gandhi looked at me and smirked, while others probably thought of me as a circus stuntman!

As the ceremonies started and people started to pay respect to the departed, I stood on the sixth step of my ladder, and started taking clear top-angle clicks and recorded the whole process with clarity and an aerial angle.

Soon, I felt some imbalance on the ladder and realised that a huge crowd of cameramen were jostling to climb up the ladder.

I laughed and jokingly told them that using the ladder would not come for free.

Mrs Indira Gandhi chuckled and said, 'Deepak, this is your ladder of success!'

Often, I carried that ladder when I travelled with Indira Gandhi, and also with Rajiv Gandhi, especially if I had to cover events like that one.

I accompanied Rajiv Gandhi and Sonia Gandhi when they visited Jordan to meet King Hussain and Crown Prince Hassan to demonstrate India's solidarity to resolve the Arab-Israeli conflict.

Politically, it was a tough issue, but individually, it was a tough one for me as well, because they would go different ways, with Rajiv meeting dignitaries, and Sonia visiting historical sites. But I managed to juggle my way through filming them both on alternate days.

Years later, I captured the moment of Rajiv Gandhi and Sonia Gandhi's visit to the grave of Yugoslav President Josip Tito, and the tomb of the unknown hero on Avala Mountain outside Belgrade. That visit to Yugoslavia was the second stop on a ten-day tour that began with a three-day stop in Amman, Spain, and Turkey.

Through my camera eyepiece, I watched carefully and took zoom and pull-outs, panning left-to-right, and right-to-left shots of them being escorted by Yugoslav officials to the White Palace Guest House in Belgrade.

This film on Rajiv Gandhi's diplomatic mission to multiple states for talks on bilateral co-operation and international issues was titled *Friendship all the Way,* and was photographed, produced, and directed by me.

In the summer of 1988, Rajiv Gandhi and Sonia Gandhi were scheduled for a four-day state visit to China, the third biggest nation in the world. It was the first in thirty-four years to be undertaken by an Indian Prime Minister.

Hailed as a historic event, the visit marked a welcome turn in China-India's relations where Rajiv Gandhi took on a most challenging foreign policy task in China. He wanted to renew India's old friendship with China, looking beyond the past, to restore the relationship between the two countries to a level commensurate with the contribution that both nations together must make for a new world order. He visited *Tiāntán*, the Temple of Heaven, a masterpiece of fifteenth-century architecture, and *Chángchéng*, the Great Wall of China. The wall was 6,700 km long, with its base made of granite slabs and the top made of bricks.

I walked with hundreds of people, including the foreign delegation and Narasimha Rao in the crowd, walking with Rajiv and Sonia Gandhi on the top of the wall, filming them all.

The following day, I filmed their visit to an ancient palace complex. The palace museum had a display of imperial collections. Rajiv Gandhi had a ninety-minute discussion with the leaders of China, talking about many things, including ancient Chinese religious architecture, the pagodas, terracotta horses, and warriors of the first emperor of China, unearthed in 1974.

Titled *Towards Panchsheel*, it became the most watched documentary that I directed.

Walking besides all-powerful political people was all hunky-dory, till it was not.

Rajiv Gandhi had been receiving multiple and constant death threats.

Though it would be scary for anyone, Rajiv Gandhi did not let it disturb his state of mind or his functioning.

Once while talking with him after two unsuccessful terrorist attempts on his life, he proudly said, 'If it comes to this, I will have to die for what I believe in. I will not hesitate,' he told me.

That day, I accompanied Rajiv Gandhi on his last public meeting in May 1991, at Sriperumbudur, a village approximately 40 km from Madras. He had gone to campaign for the Sriperumbudur Lok Sabha elections as a Congress candidate.

Imitating his dress style, I was wearing similar black Gola shoes. Mine is still intact in my almirah—a historical artefact of sorts!

It was 10:20 pm on 21 May 1991. The blast happened within inches of my head, and within seconds, we had lost him. I have no words to explain how harrowing that experience was.

In the course of my work, making many types of films on adventure, feature, drama, science fiction, action, thriller, war, and sports, I made a daily close confrontation with mortality, having to deal with the ever-looming possibility of death.

I have literally brushed past death many times and have lost many close friends. But seeing Rajiv Gandhi in shreds was beyond fathoming.

Be-Mulk Nawab

My heart was broken, my spirits shattered. Plus, the office also did not seem like it was before.

Petty politics had taken over. The regality of the assignments, the poshness of the job, and the challenge of the craft was replaced by cunning strategies.

There is a saying in Hindi by Sant Rahim:

Rahiman dhāga prem kā mat todho chhitkāy
Tuute se phir nā mile mile gāñth padh jay

Rahim says that don't snap the thread of love because
it can never be the same; if at all, it will have a knot!

I guess, my thread had snapped.

Going to the office was now becoming a drudge.

The Kargil War was being fought between India and Pakistan in the Kargil district of Ladakh, then part of the Indian-administered state of Jammu and Kashmir, along the line of control in India. The conflict was referred to as Operation Vijay. I was posted from Delhi to the Jammu and Kashmir office, and was to cover the Kargil War. I reached the Field publicity office in Jammu. Bharti Vaid, the director of the field publicity department, welcomed me. 'I have made all arrangements for your stay at the officers' mess, Deepak,' she said.

As unhappy as I was to leave my family behind in Delhi, it could not have gotten better with her saying that to me with a smiling face.

Thankfully, with evolving technology, I could now use a mobile phone to communicate instead of through handwritten letters. I called up Sadhana on her cell phone, and told her that even though it was a matter of pride shooting the Indian Army flushing out the Pakistani Army, I was risking my life and wished I could stop shooting and return to Delhi.

As always, my family became my oxygen. My soulmate, my better half, Sadhana, and my own personal South Pole, my starry-eyed ball of energy, my darling daughter Dhruvee, helped me develop a realistic sense of myself and my place in the world.

By now I had photographed over two hundred documentaries on Eastman colour in 35 mm/16 mm format and videos; directed and photographed over sixty films; produced, directed and photographed over forty films besides covering hundreds of news stories in India and abroad for Indian News Review.

I was a senior member of the Western India Cinematographer's Association—Senior Grade-2215, Mumbai, and a member of the largest professional body of working journalists engaged in visual media—the Working News Cameraman Association, New Delhi. I was accredited with the Press Information Bureau of India, and with Doordarshan as a news stringer. I had won numerous awards at different platforms in India, and had travelled to more than eighty-seven countries across the globe. The length of the film reel that I would have consumed was good enough to wrap the earth around twice!

Dhruvee was growing up fast. Her toothy smile, her exuberance, and her readiness to take on challenges bigger than her size were traits identical to mine. She was my pride.

Once, when I asked what she would like to become when she grew up, she was crystal-clear in her answer: 'Dadda I want to become an actress!' Indeed, she was ideal actress material—never camera shy, ever ready to pose and full of ideas for different filming angles. Definitely, she had got her fascination for the film world through blood. Like daddy, like daughter.

She was a very smart, understanding, and expressive child, and would watch me handle my cameras and lights, clean my camera lenses, and see how I maintained my shooting equipment. She would ask umpteen questions about my work, and it felt really good to explain the nitty-gritties of photography to her curious mind. I never felt the need for a boy. Dhruvee completed me and the family, perfectly.

I took care to nourish and nurture her dream of becoming an actress by bringing acting accessories from my foreign visits—like artificial hair, nails, dresses, and foreign film magazines with tips and tricks of the trade. I made sure that she did not have to jump boundary walls like I had done clandestinely to get exposure to her passion.

In my idle hours or on holidays, I would take them both out to the Rashtrapati Bhavan or to Lodhi Gardens and take their pictures. I loved taking Dhruvee's pictures as she was growing up, characterised by her different physical, emotional, and social changes.

She was a fantastic model for all the pictures I wanted to take.

Photography technologies were changing so fast too, and I purchased a KUBB 88 camera complete with a TTL prism,

30 mm Kodak 8, and early-type film back. It had a snappy shutter and had the perfect speed. It was a medium-format film camera with 6x6 cm square-format interchangeable lenses and a waist-level viewfinder.

I loved it and used it for a few months, but soon it was time to buy the next one in the market.

The VIVITAR V3000S was announced as the best in a popular photography magazine. It was a fully manual 35 mm film camera. I was happy with its fully manual shutter and state-of-art features.

A photographer's daughter must have photographic evidence of her life's sequel, and so I clicked as many pictures of Dhruvee as I could.

I took pictures of Sadhana too, but she always complained that I took more of Dhruvee's pictures than hers.

Women, I tell you! But to be honest, we men are no less at jealousy.

My world was a happy place. We would often go out to watch movies and eat lavish dinners. The Meridian and The Ashoka Hotel were our frequent visiting spots. To eat tandoori Indian food, I would take them to this really nice rustic-chic space called Bukhara at the ITC hotel.

The open kitchen there was the best. All three of us were true foodies.

I loved to eat and cook too. I cooked well—food, as well as stories.

But I didn't get many chances at home due to the nature of my job and the fact that Sadhana was the best cook ever.

My reduced interest in spending hours in the office became a boon for Dhruvee, as I could spend more time with her and help her try different hobbies. I wanted her to excel in studies as well as extracurriculars, not like me, who was an 'outstanding student,'—always standing outside the classroom as punishment for this prank or that.

She took some classes in classical music, kathak dance, skating, and swimming classes.

As a matter of fact, I had thrown Dhruvee straight into the swimming pool when she was only eleven months old. Of course, I jumped right after her and kept her afloat. Now, she was a beautiful swimmer. We would all go for a swim at the Lodhi Hotel.

I even taught her how to knot a tie, even though women don't really wear them, but so what!

If she had to be an actress, she must be versatile. So, the other thing I taught her was to whistle loudly, placing two fingers in the mouth, curling the tongue.

I used to whistle like that to call out to others while on expeditions. I passed it on to Dhruvee, just like many skills my Papa passed on to me.

I had one regret: that I could not take Sadhana on my foreign missions. Back then, I was like a horse with blinkers, never seeing beyond my government duties and passion for my trade.

I would write to her and keep in touch regularly, but did not take her. She too never insisted as such. The time of my foreign visits was the time of her family visits in Bengali Market.

Dhruvee would refer to Sadhana's mother's house, as '*Nani* house'! Their house was near the famous North Indian snacks and sweets shop called Bengali Sweet House and Nathu's Sweets, famous for *chana bhatura* (chickpea and fried bread snack).

My mother-in-law, Kamini Mathur, was a very sweet-natured, beautiful, calm, and hard-working person who had taken up a job with the Indian Railways as a senior language translation officer after Sadhana lost her father at a very young age.

The Railway had allotted a huge residential property, D37, with a beautiful front and back garden full of blooming flowers. The backyard also had a huge mango tree loaded with mangoes when in season, and grape climbers over the walls of the house loaded with grapes. It was very peaceful paradise, amidst the chaos of Delhi.

Sadhana was a sister to three angelic brothers: Anoop, Praveen, and Nitin—all of them extremely intelligent and family-oriented. Anoop *dada* was married to the love of his life, his college flame, Preeti. She was well-spoken and always on the run. Praveen *dada* married a petite computer engineer and homemaker, Sangeeta *Bhabhi,* and Nitin tied the knot with Lovely. Lovely was also working for the Indian Railways.

It was a good arrangement because they were with family, and I did not have to worry about them while I was away. I was also quite popular among her family and cousins. Mona, Sandeep, and Balram would be eager to listen to my adventure stories and experiences. We would discuss cars, cameras, sports, food and politics with everyone over a nice lunch meal and evening snacks prepared by Sangeeta *Bhabhi*.

Spending time with them all in Delhi would also remind me of my brothers Kiran and Anand in Mumbai. They were both married by now, and all three of us had multicultural women in our lives.

Delhi and Mumbai are within India, but life always kept coming in between, and we could meet only during summer vacations or on very special occasions.

Mumbai and Delhi's cultures are quite different. In Delhi, people loved inviting everyone home for a cosy meal and extended hospitality, unlike in Mumbai, where inviting people home was not trendy.

I had been pestering Anand for a long time to come along with Papa to Delhi and visit me, but it didn't happen for a long time. Finally, he did manage to take a break and bring his wife, Geeta, and son, Sunny, to Delhi. It was their first trip to the north, and I wanted it to be a memorable one. And it went very well with papa very impressed with my official stature, peaceful home front and respectful in-laws.

Sadhana was a fantastic host as she loved to take care of guests. Her mutton *biryani* was a superhit among all her dishes.

Food has always had great importance for me. I did not come from a poor family, but it was definitely a very traditional one. As a result, growing up, my exposure was restricted to a few gifts of nature. I had good wholesome, tasty meals, and lots of potatoes as my mother loved cooking them with everything.

With this desire to taste variety, I always wanted to be a perfect host and Sadhana agreed with me.

My house had a ready spread of food like a Roman emperor! It was my rule that anyone who came to our house should always feel welcome and cared for, especially my staff.

My motto was: 'Stay calm, work hard and party harder!'

My colleagues, A K Singh, Shyam Sundar, and Sundar Singh, office boys, my friends, visitors, and workers like gardeners, and handymen were all served food, snacks, and soft drinks, depending on the time of the day. My office did not provide any food allowance for all the shootings I did, and I always spent from my own pocket. My senior ex-chief sound recordist, D S Saini used to call me, '*Be-mulk nawab.*'

Not only my office people, but my friends too loved visiting my home. My friendships generally lasted long.

Alkesh Shah was my neighbour in Nagardas Road in Andheri, and my childhood friend. Our friendship was not just of causal acquaintances. It was what we call in Hindi '*daant kaati roti khana*' (so intimate that we shared bread).

I was a firm believer in the saying 'Tell me who your friends are, and I will tell you who YOU are,' suggesting that people you associate with can reflect your own character, values and behaviours.

Alkesh was very hard-working, an extreme foodie, and a go-getter. His motto in life was to never give up. His mind was always filled with new business ideas. We had literally grown up together and were partners in many quirky acts, like picking watches and clothes from shipping containers holding custom goods at the Mumbai port and selling them door to door at very cheap rates.

That way, we would make quick cash and instantly spend it in air-conditioned movie halls.

Alkesh's spirit for adventure was way more than mine, as he would gatecrash into weddings to eat food, pretending to be an invitee. He moved to Delhi once I moved here, and I would listen to his daring tales with amusement.

I knew we were '*lambi race ke ghode* (horses meant for long races)'; in this case, a lifelong bond.

He married a homely, well-educated journalist called Jyotsna. Thankfully, Sadhana gelled well with her; in fact, she was very nice to all my friends and their families.

As I said earlier, Sadhana and I loved having guests for dinners, lunches, brunches, short stays, and even long stays.

I loved surrounding myself with people who had great qualities, great humour, great stories, and above all, great appetites!

Good friends are like rare gems, and I had a bagful of

such gems. These friendships developed when our families, and our kids were growing up, and are still going strong. Our relocation to Gurgaon only made the desire to meet and spend time together even stronger.

Sharawati, my friend from the mountaineering expedition, was a frequent visitor. She and her husband, Douglas Keith Scott, a British mountaineer, who was on the team which had the first ascent on the southwest face of Mount Everest on 24 September 1975 would often pass through Delhi *en route* to their next venture.

We loved having them over, listening to their new adventures as they devoured Sadhana's delicious *parathas* (fried flatbreads). Doug loved Sadhana's mango pickle chutney and would not only eat here but also take packets back home.

Col Somveer Mundalia and his family were another example of our deep and long-lasting friendship. He was in the Indian Army, and we would often go for army dinners to the DSOI club. My daughter and their kids grew up together.

Dr Shastri and his family is yet another example of friendships that know no age boundaries. It is fed with a genuine connection. He was our neighbour, and we called on him looking for medicines for little Dhruvee's cough and cold and became friends for life and beyond. After Dr Shastri's untimely demise, his family retained the connection; Sadhana and his wife, Vijay Laxmi, became very close friends, always hanging out together, shopping together, and gossiping together.

Her daughter, Dr Anamika, was also a great companion, but that friendship took a magical turn once she left India and travelled the world.

Family is given to us by destiny, but friends are the family we choose for ourselves.

Anamika became that friend-turned-family for us, making sure to spend good quality time with us in Gurgaon whenever she visited India.

She had this talent for language and could connect with any age group. She could sit with Sadhana and talk about miscellaneous things, then sit with Dhruvee and be that big sister-cum-friend, and be with me and guzzle loads of beer and talk about things scientific or technical.

Whenever she stayed with us in Gurgaon, I could not wait for her to return home after her shopping for a chilled beer-drinking and chatting session, enjoying her witty discussions. I could talk my heart out because she was not judgemental.

Sadhana and Dhruvee loved her very much, too. She clearly had made a lasting impression of love upon us.

Kids grow too fast. My little princess was now all grown up, and finished her graduation in journalism, and a Master's in Political Science. Needless to say, she took up my legacy and started her own career in the media by joining the popular American news channel, CNN. She would work very hard, working full time at CNN, while honing her skills to launch herself into her childhood passion, acting. She took classes to learn various dictions, improvisation techniques, dialogue delivery and powerful emoting.

***

Giving importance to the relationship and harmony I have with myself and my personal well-being, I started driving my life in cruise mode—meandering through, enjoying life, taking things at a slower pace, and taking up only those projects which kindled my passion.

I took up an eight-episode project with Doordarshan, titled *Namaskar Kalakar*.

It was a tribute to great Indian master painters like Raja Ravi Varma, M F Hussain, Kulkarni, Laxman Pai, Sosa David, Aparna Kaur, and S K Aryan. By the finish of the shoot, I had gotten so well-versed in art that with just a glance at a painting, I could tell who the painter was!

I also did a film on the launching of hot air balloons and fly ash management.

The world of cinematography had evolved, and so did I. It was the digital beta and U-matic era. The transition from film to digital was a revolution, and I embraced it wholeheartedly. While purists debated its merits, I saw it as an opportunity—an era where storytelling could reach more people, where young filmmakers could create without the constraints of expensive film reels.

My name was getting recognised as an expert in aerial filming and shooting in snow-bound regions at minus temperatures; and in desert regions at plus temperatures; shooting on high seas and at high-altitudes, creating night effects, table tops and miniatures, special effects, and fiction.

I got an anonymous call asking me to do a film on the Kailash Manasarovar, the Kailash range considered to be most sacred by Hindus. Its highest peak, the 6,675 m high Kailash Parbat, was said to be the holy residence of Lord Shiva and Goddess Parvati.

I had just completed *Namaskar Kalakar* and was already inspired by great paintings of gods and goddesses. So, it sounded like a perfect film, like the earlier ones on great expeditions.

'Who is the producer?' I asked.

'*Yogi raj* Amar Jyoti Shyam *ji* is producing the film. He

takes his followers every year up to the top, and wants to film it this year,' he replied.

'Brilliant! Please arrange a meeting with him. I will let you know my decision after that,' I told him.

Yogi raj Amar Jyoti *Maharaj* was a spiritual guru and had a meditation centre in Palampur. He was considered a *Satguru*, or true *guru* in the ancient tradition of teachers of mankind.

I decided to do the film after meeting him. He looked pristine and pure in his spotless white robes, and our discussion was very soothing and inspiring. He held my hand and politely spoke at length about various things. Interested in photography himself, we spoke about camera equipment, filming costs, budgeting and travel plans.

I found myself surrounded by a very supportive and talented team that worked for Swami *ji,* and I soon became everybody's favourite during the ascent.

On the second day of the pilgrimage, I looked through my viewfinder and filmed appropriate shots, as everyone took the customary holy bath at the holy Sheshnag Lake.

As we ascended higher, the white tip of Mount Kailash emanated!

There was a surreal, lingering feeling as the surroundings were very still. No one spoke a word. The blue waters were calm, the white mountaintops, serene, as if I was looking at a heavenly picture like the ones made by those great artists like Raja Ravi Varma. I felt completely mesmerised, and a deep inner calm descended over me.

The rough pathways and uphill walk towards the lake became easy.

Swamiji was so inquisitive about filmmaking that he asked,

'Deepak *ji, kya mai apka* camera *chala sakta hun?* (Deepak *ji*, can I use your camera?)'

'*Han, han, kyu nahi?* (Of course, why not?)' I was surprised at my own ease at sharing my camera, something that I am quite possessive about!

'I will buy an ARRIFLEX camera to be used only by you. We will make many more films together,' he said in admiration.

Soon, we reached the magnificent Manasarovar Lake. I took the pictures and videos from many angles, capturing many beautiful shades of the environment.

Then, bowing to my destiny, I dipped my feet in the holy water and paid homage to the Almighty.

We all then went to the Ravan *Taal*, adjacent to Manasarovar, known as the abode of Ravana, the demon king, and also a great devotee of Lord Shiva. People generally label it as an unholy lake, but I could feel the purity in this place and spent some time there.

Undertaking a yatra to Kailash Manasarovar was an epic experience. I felt immense gratitude towards the Almighty and for Swami *ji*.

The Last Shot, A New Beginning

This story, my story, I know is for those who dare to dream, who refuse to give up, and who believe that with enough courage, even the impossible can be possible.

I needed to turn the tide. By now, I was driven to turn it, and so, I leaped into the deep end to try something only a few cinematographers would do. I opened my own production house by the name of Filmsmith's. I was determined to build on it, and take it as far as I could.

I continued to develop my filming skills, make bold, dangerous choices and work almost non-stop. Success means different things for different people; some measure it in the form of awards, and some in the form of money and financial status. For me success meant being able to bring good food to eat on my plate; to be able to do whatever I wanted and whenever I wanted it.

I could see my popularity grow. Iconic, isn't it, that after deciding to quit the Films Division, I had come so far in deciding and producing my own films under my own home banner? Though I was integrally still connected with the Government of India, where they wanted my production house, Filmsmith's to make films on field publicity. They wanted me to make films to educate the public, promote participation in development activities and provide a forum for people to express their views through my films. I made films on subjects like polio and AIDS. My films *Janjal, Amanat, Paigam, Asha Ki Kiran* were fiction films directed and photographed by me. All of these films were also dubbed in over twenty languages by me, and used as key propaganda material by the Government of India.

I always had a natural knack for learning languages. I could fluently speak English, Punjabi, Sanskrit, French, Nepali, Kannada, Marathi, and Hindi. This deep love for languages eventually led me to film projects, where I began dubbing in multiple languages. Over time, I went on to dub numerous films across different languages, turning my passion into a fulfilling creative pursuit.

Dr Jagdish Gupta was an Indian poet and served as the Chairman of the Department of Hindi at Allahabad University. A close family friend of my mother-in-law, he played a significant role in encouraging me to take up Hindi language–based film projects, recognizing my aptitude and passion for languages.

Dr Gupta introduced me to Virendra Mishra, a poet at heart and a seasoned news commentator for Doordarshan who soon became my trusted voice. His narration and dubbing brought life to several of my films, making him my go-to voicing artist.

Filmsmith's also produced a popular talk show *Live Wire* for DD Metro, and several short films on extraordinary subjects like Chilka Lake—the wonder lagoon on the birds of Chilka, global warming, maritime heritage, and on the Bajaj motorcycle rally to Siachen Glacier.

My life after these last few projects had pivoted outside

the Films Division. I was now doing a lot of work in different spheres—regional shows for regional channels like *Harfan Maula, Kursi Boldi Hai* and *Insaaf* for the Srinagar channel; dozens of audio visuals for corporates; commercial documentaries on East End Foods, the largest Asian food chain in the United Kingdom; and films on social causes like the *Project Bhavana* for Delhi State Industrial Development and Energy and Resources Institute (TERI), so much so that the Films Division was taking a back seat. I had to keep pitching myself at the Films Division for more recognition in terms of acknowledgements and promotions. I would spend hours and hours only fighting for allowances for my foreign travels and unwanted transfer postings. Office politics and correspondence with senior office officials was exhausting me.

Why should I put energy into all this, I thought, especially when I was getting to do so much work outside of this government job. I, therefore, did not want to wait for retirement, and decided to take voluntary retirement. I thought I would gain considerable momentum in paving the way for more offers to come my way and finally quit the Films Division.

I was always a lone ranger; plenty of people focussed on me and approached me for my ability to shoot good films and connect with the audience. I collaborated with Rama Pandey on producing a serial *Shabash Begum* and I did many other television serials like *Chehre, Meetha Zahar, and Harfan Maula.* This less travelled road to the world of television serials was a total standout. I was blessed to have my associate Rajesh Gandhi, art designer Kedaram Vishwanathan, editor Rajeev Sharma, and commentator Pradeep Kumar—a team of extremely talented and efficient men who made it easier for me to complete projects on time. All of them are now heading eminent departments in the media industry.

I shot many feature films as well, and I remember it was *Champaran Ke Gaon* that became my most memorable one. It was to be shot in a remote village in Bihar, where burglars and dacoits roamed freely. The film had Padma Khanna, an Indian actress and dancer, most remembered for her role as the heroine in the film *Saudagar* with Amitabh Bachchan. I had also worked with her in *Pakeezah* where she had body-doubled for Meena Kumari and helped complete the film.

The film had an item number, a live dance sequence to be shot with real people from the village in the audience. I adjusted the Hydrargyrum Medium-arc lodide light (HMI light, a type of gas discharge lamp used in films and television production, known for its bright, efficient, and daylight-balanced light), and asked the light man to put a baby light right behind Padma's head as a backlight, giving the effect of a halo.

In different situations, I would play with the source lights available and could easily light up with just one single baby light.

While she stood there memorising her dance steps, I quickly went ahead with my light meter. I set the light meter ISO to the same as my camera and decided on the aperture. I was getting multiple readings in different areas of my frame, which was good. I was very fond of my SEKONIC light meter. It was by a Japanese manufacturer, and the light meter was known for its accuracy, versatility, and durability. With my SEKONIC light meter, I could easily measure the light falling on the subject even from a distance, and it helped me ensure that the colours captured on my camera are true to life.

I would go by the Sunny Sixteen rule in photography—a photography rule of thumb that helps you get good exposures in bright sunny conditions without a light meter by changing shutter speeds by guesswork, depending on how cloudy or sunny the day is.

Ever since I had gotten into medium format photography, I knew at some point that I would need a light meter. When I was shooting a lot of my photos on 35 mm film, most of my cameras such as the PENTAX K 1000, had a built-in light meter or some form of light meter on them, and I felt that my photos exposed just right so I never felt the need to buy an external light meter.

I knew I was going to invest in a more expensive medium-format camera. I felt it was essential for me to get a light meter so I could do the camera justice, and get the best photos possible.

In the early 1980s, I would use the WESTON MASTER IV and V light meters that came with an Inver cone. These were British-made, and had selenium light cells. When I bought it, I was over the moon!

How time had flown, and I had jumped on from WESTON light meter ranges to SEKONIC light meters.

I enjoyed making films on infrequent subjects and added another feather to my cap, when at the behest of a dear friend, Bipin Chaubal, I made another film on ambidextrous people and the film was titled *विलक्षण प्रतिभा-amazing talent.*

With every film I did, I would be adding more tools to my toolbox. I purchased expensive digital cameras and lenses, and was finding myself being more intimate with the changing world of movie making. My romance with my cameras continued and I gained many professional relationships.

My old friends and fellow cinematographers, Ajit Nayak, who shot the famous *Ramayana* serials and Mahesh Sinha who worked with me at the Films Division would initiate conversations where we would discuss the rapid growth in technology and how the new generation was taking over. I would think maybe if I would not have become a cinematographer, I would definitely have been in the field of aeronautics.

I also joined a production house in Delhi when Harikrit Films approached me to do a film on the famous sharp shooters of Baghpath. The film was on two old women who were popularly known as Revolver *Dadis*. The film was titled *Bonds of Baghpath*. The producer, Tarsem Antil, was the son of a colleague of mine, with whom I had made many agricultural publicity films. I love championing young talent, so his proposal appealed to me.

He and his business partner Manisha Bajaj wanted me on his consultation and advisory board. Manisha was a writer and is best known for subjective poetry programmes on television. Together we made a few films, and this association gave me a taste of being on advisory boards.

I loved it and joined a few institutes. I had fun giving lectures on photography, but also on sundry but essential topics like table manners in official gatherings, and on how to conduct oneself in formal meetings. Young boys and girls loved my overall presence, my quirky examples, my dress style, and above everything, the insight I gave into the world of political leaders that they could not have gotten elsewhere.

UNICEF invited me to attend several workshops on photography, and I also reviewed film cameras and films.

Philanthropy was always close to my heart, and I was a great supporter of women's rights. Having two strong women at home (Dhruvee and Sadhana), a strong woman to look up to (Indira Gandhi), and a strong woman to admire (my mother), I was always ready to make films on issues that were often overlooked.

The only thing that I regretted was that after starting my career with Nariman A Irani, and working in big-banner commercial films, my life never allowed me to take a turn back towards mainstream cinema. I guess it could have been because of my decision to move base from Mumbai to Delhi. Mumbai, is where the film industry in India began in the early twentieth century, due to its colonial and economic infrastructure. Had I remained in Mumbai, life could have taken that turn, but then again, if you want to make God laugh, you only have to tell him your plans, it is believed. God, though, has been very kind to me.

One day in 2018, I met Swati Bedekar. She was instrumental, along with her husband, in making a unique machine to make sanitary napkins. They were not only generating employment, but also bringing awareness about female hygiene.

With my new CANON EOS 5D MARK IV DSLR, a professional-grade 30.4-megapixel full-frame digital single-lens reflex camera and the most powerful and versatile cinema camera with a large-format global shutter and ground-breaking latest technology, the RED KOMODO 6 K camera, I reached out to her.

Together, we made a film touching upon issues like normal conversations about this natural female process, easy access to napkins, and their proper disposal.

The film was titled *Dignity Hygiene made Affordable Worldwide*.

In the beginning of 2015, I went to Mumbai to prepare to make a film on the topic of waste material, titled *Kachrey se Kanchan*. Dhruvee had moved to Mumbai, and I would often visit her. This is when I had decided to make this film.

I went to the local municipal office to get permission from the commissioner to shoot in slums.

He listened to me, and then putting his head back into

his papers, said nonchalantly, 'Why don't you give an *arzi* (application) and come back in two to four months? I will see what can be done.'

'I have come from Delhi, Sir, and I wanted to do the film now,' I replied politely. I was frustrated, though.

A lady was seated there, and she beckoned me to the side. She was Seema Raidkar, an Officer on Special Duty (OSD) at the Mumbai Municipal Corporation. She said that I could shoot without any permission.

She said, 'What do you want to shoot? I will take you with me; you won't need any permissions.'

Together, we went to different locations in Mumbai, like Dharavi and the villages around, which had mountains of filth.

She also told me that there are a few localities around, like Khar Dhanda, which do not even have a toilet, a basic human right, and asked if I could consider filming that. I immediately agreed.

After coming home, I sat and thought it over.

With a camera on my shoulder and compassion in my heart, I conceptualised and wrote the script. Then I called up a senior actress friend, Sunita Shirole, and asked her if she would like to do some pro bono work for me, as it was a self-budgeted film.

She agreed readily, though she confessed she felt uncomfortable walking on the beaches. Since those scenes were vital to the film, I took an executive call and recreated a beach-like ambience right outside her house in Malad. But we soon ran into an unexpected imbroglio while shooting with the local residents. When they learned what the film was about, it reopened old emotional wounds. Tempers flared, and the crowd turned riotous. The situation quickly descended into vandalism. Their reaction, I felt, was justified, and I found myself at a complete loss for any logic or reason that could pacify them. We could barely manage the situation and could resume shooting only when Dhruvee reached there, and the crowd recognised her!

Oh, I didn't tell you, did I?

Dhruvee had shifted to Mumbai to pursue a career in acting, and had become a well-known television presenter and actor. She had anchored several shows on television and acted in many serials, including the most popular Balaji Films.

I was proud of her because while emceeing for big corporate shows, she could face more than twenty live cameras that were usually set up and talk extempore for hours. She was so proficient in managing her diction and accent according to the requirements of the business house, moving from British and American accents to Marathi or Gujarati accents!

Always being a man behind the lens, I was quite shy of facing the camera myself, so I was very happy and kind of surprised to see Dhruvee's talent, which was an offshoot from mine, but unique to her.

Years before, my heart had sunk when she had declared that she was moving to Mumbai. But she had made a name for herself without any mentor, patron, or chaperone. She worked extremely hard in an industry known for its nepotism, its favouritism, and its clandestine manipulations.

She started by accepting smaller roles and moved on to play many lead characters in numerous television shows. She kept herself completely focussed and reminded me of my immersive shooting experiences.

Because of her TV gigs, she had become a household face, and when she reached the site of the shooting, the angry mob instantly recognised her and heard our reason for filming.

We finished the shooting, and the film was named *Mala*

Laaj Vatat Nahi (I am not Ashamed). I had purposefully named it such to bring out the satire. My childhood friend Harish Bhimani, with whom I grew up from the third standard during the early days after moving to Andheri—taking pictures, developing an eye for composition with our very prestigious early box camera, and getting into new mischief—went on to become a celebrated voice artist and the iconic narrator of the television series Mahabharata. It was a profound privilege that he recorded the narration for my film.

I had close contacts with all the Prime Ministers of India, from Indira Gandhi, Rajiv Gandhi, P V Narasimha Rao, Atal Bihari Vajpayee, Manmohan Singh and Narendra Modi. Out of all of them, I found Narendra Modi to be the strongest. I sent the film to him, and he summoned me and deputed Dr Jitendra Singh, Minister of State for Personnel, Public Grievances and Pensions of India, to see what could be done.

Heeding my request and with the intervention of the Prime Minister, within twenty days, toilets were made for them!

The film also got a national award.

You must be wondering about my next project! Which adventure, which expedition, which ascent did I embark on?

Well, for two or three days, I was feeling some discomfort in my body. When things didn't normalise after home remedies, Sadhana suggested that we should visit a doctor.

Reluctantly, I agreed.

The next day, I got up, shaved, dressed nicely and stepped down from our second floor house to go to a nearby hospital with Sadhana.

The doctor checked me and asked in shock, 'How come you came walking in? You have suffered a major heart attack!'

I smiled and said, 'Sir, you don't know. I have done bigger

stunts in my past. This is nothing.'

But to be honest, I, too, was shocked—a heart attack and me? I was hale and hearty. What had happened, and when and how?

They operated upon me as an emergency, but on the operating table, my heart developed a rare condition, and they could not revive my heart.

Yes, you have guessed right.

I am no more.

I died on that table.

Every story has an ending, and so did mine. But an ending is merely a transition to something new.

As Lord Krishna said in the *Shrimad Bhagavad Gita*:

Verse 2.22

Nainaṁ chindanti śastrāṇi nainaṁ dahati pāvakaḥ
na cainaṁ kledayanty āpo na śoṣayati mārutah'

The soul cannot be pierced by weapons, burned by fire,
moistened by water, or withered by the wind.

I have died, but I am not dead.

My journey, my battles, my triumphs—they live on through the frames I have captured, through the stories I have told. And most importantly, through Dhruvee.

Verse 2.27

Jātasya hi dhruvo mṛtyur dhruvaṁ janma mṛtasya ca. tasmād
aparihārye 'rthe na tvaṁ śocitum arhasi

Death is certain for one who has been born, and
rebirth is inevitable for one who has died.
Therefore, you should not lament over the inevitable.

I strongly believe that we are given this human life to make the best out of our lives' journeys.

I lived mine. Lived for myself and for all those around me. Now is your time.

I was a cameraman, so my advice to you, my Dear Reader, is:

Aspire to pick up a camera and dream of creating something meaningful.

The world is your canvas. Paint it with light, shadow, and emotion. Chase the impossible, and when you do, capture it.

For in the end, it is not just about the images we create but the lives we touch through them.

I held forth my story—**'Recount, Rehearse, Unfold.'**

Lights, Camera, Action.

And now, it is yours to unfold further.

A small selection from the hundreds of letters, invitations, certificates, and souvenirs he received in his lifetime.

The Government of Kenya

has the pleasure in inviting

MR. D.R. HALDNKAR

to a Reception

in honour of

The Heads of State and Delegates attending

The U. N. Conference on New and Renewable Sources of Energy

at Parliament Buildings

on Monday, 10th August, 1981, 6.30 p.m. to 9.30 p.m.

R.S.V.P.
Chairman/Hospitality Sub-committee
K.I.C. Tel. 332383 Ext. 2181 or 2193

(PLEASE BRING THIS CARD WITH YOU)

The Government of Kenya invites heads of state and delegates to a reception in honour of attendees of the UN Conference on New and Renewable Sources of Energy

TO MEET THE MEMBERS OF THE INDIAN EVEREST EXPEDITION '84

Lieut Gen (Retd) A M Sethna
PVSM, AVSM

Chairman

India Tourism Development Corporation

request the pleasure of the company of

~~Smt.~~ Shri Deepak Haldankar

at Lunch

on 8 June 84 *at* 1.00 PM

at Ashok Hotel, New Delhi

RSVP
Tel ~~373837~~ ...57

Invitation to meet the members of the 1984 Indian Everest Expedition at a lunch hosted by the Tourism Development Corporation

सत्यमेव जयते

The Prime Minister

requests the pleasure of the company of

Mr. D. R. Haldankar

at the Concluding Ceremony of the
Fourth Meeting of the Summit Level Group for
South - South Consultation and Cooperation (G-15)
on Wednesday, the 30th March, 1994
at 4.30 p.m. at Vigyan Bhavan.

Regrets only
301 7020 / 301 7327

Invitation is non-transferable.
Please bring this card with you.

Invitation from the Prime Minister for the concluding ceremony of G-15

In honour of H.E. the President of India.

सत्यमेव जयते

The High Commissioner for India
and Mrs. Seyid Muhammad
request the pleasure of the company of

Shri D.R. Haldankar

at Reception *on* Thursday, the 30th July, 1981
at 9, Kensington Palace Gardens, W8 4QP *at* 4.00 to 6.00 PM.

Dress: National/Lounge Suit

R.S.V.P.—PRIVATE SECRETARY,
INDIA HOUSE, ALDWYCH
LONDON, WC2B 4NA
PHONE : 836-2556

Invitation from the High Commissioner of India and Mrs Seyid Muhammad to a royal reception at Kensington Palace Gardens

Little White Book with Golden Emblem

RESTRICTED

सत्यमेव जयते

VISIT

OF

SHRI N. SANJIVA REDDY

President of the Republic of India

TO

LONDON

(United Kingdom)

FROM

Monday, 27th July, 1981/Sravana 5, 1903 (Saka)

TO

Saturday, 1st August, 1981/Sravana 10, 1903 (Saka)

RESTRICTED

31

India No. 5— 1. Shri K. S. Sastry,
Private Secretary to the President.
2. Shri Kula Nand, Valet.
3. Shri K. Hanumanthu, Valet.
4. Shri Dev Narain, Valet.

India No. 6— Shri R. D. Sathe,
Foreign Secretary,
Ministry of External Affairs.

India No. 7— 1. Shri W. Lazarus,
Principal Information Officer, PIB.
2. Shri K. Suryanarayana.
Press Secretary to the President.
3. Shri T. S. Ashok,
Photographic Officer (*Front Seat*).

India No. 8— 1. Shri M. H. Ansari,
Chief of Protocol.
Ministry of External Affairs.
2. Shri S. D. Trivedi,
Director, Ministry of Home Affairs.

India No. 9— 1. Shri Y. D. Kadolkar,
Cameraman, Doordarshan.
2. Shri R. M. Sathe,
Sound Recordist, Doordarshan.

32

India No. 10.— 1. Shri Suresh Chopra,
Correspondent, AIR.
2. Shri D. R. Haldankar,
Cameraman, Films Division

India No. 11— 1. Shri Jagdish Prasad,
Section Officer (Tours).
2. Shri M. L. Tiwari,
Technical Assistant.

सत्यमेव जयते

VISIT OF
SHRI RAJIV GANDHI
PRIME MINISTER OF INDIA
AND
SHRIMATI SONIA GANDHI
TO
SPAIN

15th to 17th July, 1988

Shri S. S. Pokharia

Shri Durga Prasad

Shri R. A. Parasetti

Shri M. S. Dhillon

Shri Arvind Mishra

Shri V. R. C. Nathan

Shri Nain Singh

Shri Rai Das

Shri Rajesh Singh

15

OFFICIAL MEDIA

Shri Amitabh Chakravarty
Doordarshan

Shri R. K. Padmanaban
Doordarshan

Shri Suresh Behr
Doordarshan

Shri Mohinder Singh
Doordarshan

Shri Radha Nath Chaturvedi
All India Radio

Shri Jaswant Rai
All India Radio

Shri D. R. Haldenkar
Films Division

Shri V. K. Shyam Sunder
Films Division

Shri P. K. Kapur
Photo Division

Shri Manbir Singh
X. P. Division

16

Team-signed photograph on Mount Everest

MC Productions
MOTION PICTURE PRODUCERS

PHONE : 366344

93, WARDEN ROAD,
"BEACH VIEW"
BOMBAY-26.

Date 26th Sept., '62

TO WHOM SOEVER IT MAY CONCERN

This is to certify that Shri Deepak Kumar R. Haldankar is working with me as an assistant cameraman for the last three years and at present is assisting me in the movie 'Wasiat' being produced by Shri Manu Narang.

I found him to be trust worthy, hard working and very enthusiatic.

I wish him success in his future career.

Nariman Irani

NARIMAN A IRANI W.I.C.A.

Certificate of Appreciation from Nariman A Irani (Wasiyat)

RALHAN
PRODUCTIONS

16th September 1969.

TO WHOMSOEVER IT MAY CONCERN

This is to certify that Shri Deepak kumar R. Haldankar, is working in our Production as an assistant camera man with our camera man Shri Nariman A. Irani, for the last three years. During his course of work I found him to be honest, hardworking and very enthusiatic.

I look forward a bright future in him and wish him every success.

for RALHAN PRODUCTIONS,

Gopal Ralhan

Gopal Ralhan

(PRODUCTION CONTROLLER

Nariman Irani

(Nariman A. Irani W.I.C.A.)

217-C Famous Cine Building, Mahalaxmi, Bombay-11 Phone : 372971 & 379331-22 Grams : RALHANPRO

Certificate of Appreciation from Nariman A Irani, 1969

phone:
office: 440398
res. 523221
MOTION PICTURES PRODUCE

NS FILM

Shree Sound Studios,
goculdas pasta road, Dadar,
B O M B A Y.1

September 13, 1969.

TO WHOM IT MAY CONCERN

This is to certify that Mr.Deepak Kumar Haldankar has been working as an Assistant to our Chief Cameraman Mr.Nariman Ir in our under production movie "MAH-RAJA" in Eastman Color.

for N.S.FILM,

PROPIETOR

NUTAN SANJAY
NARESH SAIGAL'S
MAH-RAJA
eastmancolor
music MADAN MOHAN

Certificate of Appreciation for the film *Maharaja* – Nariman A Irani

MOVIERAMA

"MIRIAM" B/11, SITLADEVI TEMPLE ROAD, MAHIM, BOMBAY-16 PHONE : 454619

12th September 69.

To whom it may concern.

This is to certify that Shri Deepak Haldankar was working in my film "MOJI GORCAN" as an assistant camera man. During his course of work, I found him to be honest, hard working and very much enthusiastic.

I look forward a bright future in him and wish him every success.

ASalam.

Certificate from A Salam for Moji Gorcan, 1969

WORKING NEWS CAMERAMEN'S ASSOCIATION

(Registered under the Societies Registration Act)
C/o 58, Janpath, New Delhi-110001

Tel. No. 3321385

June 19, 2001

TO WHOM IT MAY CONCERN

Mr. Deepak Haldankar is a member of WORKING NEWS CAMERAMEN'S ASSOCIATION, the largest professional body of working journalists engaged in visual media. He is a bonafide professional news cameraman of repute. He has been working as a news cameraman for the last 25 years and has been accredited with the Press Information Bureau, Govt. Of India (Press Card no.1897)

He may kindly be extended all facilities in performing his professional duties.

Pramod Mathur
General Secretary
WORKING NEWS CAMERAMEN'S ASSOCIATION

Working News Cameraman Association—Pramod Mathur

BY DIPLOMATIC BAG

सत्यमेव जयते

S. Z. QASIM
SECRETARY

भारत सरकार
महासागर विकास विभाग
'महासागर भवन'
ब्लाक-१२, सी० जी० ओ० काम्पलैक्स,
लोधी रोड, नई दिल्ली-११०००३

GOVERNMENT OF INDIA
DEPARTMENT OF OCEAN DEVELOPMENT
'MAHASAGAR BHAVAN'
BLOCK-12, C. G. O. COMPLEX,
LODI ROAD, NEW DELHI-110003.

GRAM : MAHASAGAR
PHONE : 616874 TELEX : 031-5300 DOD-IN

DO NO. DOD/SPS-10/85
SEPTEMBER 10, 1985

My dear Deepak Haldenkar,

Thank you for your beautiful picture post-card conveying greetings and good wishes. It is nice of you to remember me from the Everest Expedition.

I wish you all good luck in your challenging task of scaling the Mount Everest. Please convey my best wishes to all the members of your team and their safe return home.

With regards,

Yours sincerely,

(S.Z. QASIM)

Mr. Deepak Haldenkar,
Indian Army Everest Expedition 1985,
C/o Embassy of India,
KATHMANDU.
(Nepal)

Letter from S Z Qasim congratulating for the Army Expedition

GOVERNMENT OF INDIA
MINISTRY OF EXTERNAL AFFAIRS

भारत सरकार
विदेश मंत्रालय, नई दिल्ली

No. V.11/403/920/74 New Delhi (11) the 25th Oct. 1982

The Ministry of External Affairs present their compliments to the High Commission for Australia in India and have the honour to state that Shri D.R. Haldankar, Newsreel officer will be proceeding to Australia to participate in the 2nd Expedition of Antarctica. It is requested that appropriate entry visa for Australia valid for entry within three months may kindly be affixed on his passport on presentation.

The Ministry avail themselves of this opportunity to renew to the High Commission the assurances of their highest consideration.

MINISTRY OF EXTERNAL AFFAIRS
GOVT. OF INDIA

The High Commission for Australia
in India, New Delhi.

Letter from the Ministry of External Affairs regarding the Antarctica expedition

Letters of information from the Department of Ocean Development and Indian Mountaineering Foundation—regarding the wellbeing and activities of the Antarctica Team.

महासागर विकास विभाग
नई दिल्ली
DEPARTMENT OF OCEAN DEVELOPMENT
South Block
New Delhi

J.L. Sarin
Director
T.No. 376689

D.O.No. DOD/21-ATCT/40/82

December 27, 1982

Dear ~~Sir~~/Madam,

This is to inform you that M.V.Polar Circle had a smooth voyage through the roaring forties. The members of the expedition were in the midst of ice bergs on Christmas day. Yesterday evening i.e. on 26th December, 1982 they were at 67°.29' South Latitude and 15°.24' East Longitude. They expect to land on Antarctica within a day or two. They will probably be on Antarctica by the time this letter reaches you.

2. All members of the team are fine and send you their best wishes for a very happy new year. Please keep sending me messages for them, as these are eagerly awaited by the members of the team and are a source of encouragement for them.

Yours sincerely,

J. L. Sarin

(J.L. Sarin)

Letter from J L Sarin, Director of Department of Ocean Development—December 1982

(13)

सत्यमेव जयते

महासागर विकास विभाग
नई दिल्ली

DEPARTMENT OF OCEAN DEVELOPMENT
South Block
New Delhi

J.L. Sarin
Director

T.No. 376689

D.O.No. DOD/21-ATCT/40/82

January 20, 1983

Dear ~~Sir~~/Madam,

The members of the Second Indian Antarctic Expedition have been in Antarctica for more than 3 weeks now. They hope to stay on for about one month more. After setting up their Base Camp, they shifted to Dakshin Gangotri which is about 80 kilo metres interior, 3 days ago. They have started making erecting their second hut at this place. Their scientific work is progressing according to schedule.

2. They met some Russian and East German scientists who were also doing scientific work near Dakshin Gangotri. They have visited the Russian station which is located in that region, and invited them to the Indian Camp for Republic Day celebrations. In addition, the Penguins are keeping them company.

3. Last week some members of the team landed on an ice berg by Naval Helicopters. They stayed on the ice berg all day and carried out scientific studies. Such studies of an ice berg have been done for the first time by Indian scientists.

4. You might have seen the stamp which was issued on 9th January, 1983 to mark the first anniversary of the landing by Indian scientists on Antarctica last year. I shall be sending you a First Day Cover issued on this occasion, with my next letter.

5. All members of the team are well and in good health.

With regards,

Yours sincerely,

J.L. Sarin

(J.L. Sarin)

Letter from J L Sarin, Director of Department of Ocean Development—January 1983

INDIAN MOUNTAINEERING FOUNDATION
Benito Juarez Road, Anand Niketan, New Delhi-110021

Cdr. Joginder Singh
Member
Sponsoring Committee

May 18, 1984

Dear Sir/Madam,

Everest Expedition News Letter No. 6.

I am sorry to inform you that Camp III set up just above the Western CWM, came under an avalanche after mid-night on May 15-16. Naib Sub N.D. Sharpa and two Nepalese Mountain Guides received injuries. Fortunatel , Lopsang Tshering and Miss Bachendri Pal had a miraculous escape.

2. The victims of the avalanche accident were brought down to Base Camp and evacuated by helicopter to Kathmandu.

3. There has been unusual bad weather in the Nepal Himalayas accompanied by heavy snowfall in the higher reaches. Climbing parties of the expedition which were on the higher camps have, therefore, been withdrawn, as is the normal practice, as a precautionary measure. They will rest and recuperate at the lower altitude. When the weather improves, the Leader will decide when to send the climbing parties up again taking into consideration all other factors.

4. All other members of the Expedition are in good health and spirit. More in our next News Letter.

With best wishes,

Yours faithfully,

Cdr. Joginder Singh

Letter from Joginder Singh—May 1984

Postcard with signatures of the Indian Antarctica Team

SECOND INDIAN SCIENTIFIC EXPEDITION

Dakshin Gangotri
ANTARCTICA

Date:

EXPLORATION ANTARCTICA

Shri V.K. Raina
Shri M.K. Kaul
Shri S.K. Chakraborty
Dr. A. Sen Gupta
Dr. P.K. Pasricha
Dr. C.R. Sreedharan
Shri A.K. Sharma
Shri Luis A.D! Cruz
Shri S.G. Prabhu Matondkar
Dr. G.S. Mittal
Shri H.R.S. Sastry
Shri D.R. Haldankar
Surg. Lt. Cdr. D.B. Rao
Lt. Cdr. R.S. Bill
Lt. Cdr. K.S. Randhawa
Lt. Cdr. Kulwant Singh
Lt. Cdr. Rajesh Sethi
Lt. Ujjal Singh
Shri B.S. Thakur
Shri I.Khan Ch. Ela
Shri Ravinder K. Kapoor
Major D.N. Singh
Major P.K. Nair
Major Jai Bahuguna
Wng. Cdr. Abhay Singh
Sqn. Ldr. H.N. Chaturvedi
Sqn. Ldr. R.S. Tandon
Shri Anant Kumar Andhare

Final list of all the team members

सत्यमेव जयते

PRIME MINISTER

New Delhi
June 27, 1985

Dear Shri Haldankar,

We had taken up the Antarctica Programme with great expectations.

I would like to have from you your assessment of your trip to the Antarctica, your personal experiences, difficulties and your suggestions for planning of future expeditions.

Yours sincerely,

Shri D.R. Haldankar,
Member,
Second Antarctica Expedition,
News Reel Officer,
Films Division, I&B,
Pandara Road,
New Delhi.

Letter from the Prime Minister—Rajiv Gandhi

Shri D.R. Haldankar,
Member,
Second Antarctica Expedition,
News Reel Officer,
Films Division, I&B,
Pandara Road,
New Delhi.

PRIME MINISTER

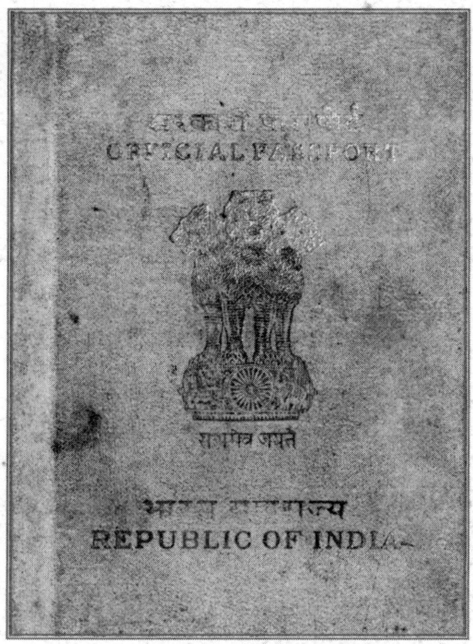

White Passport—Republic of India

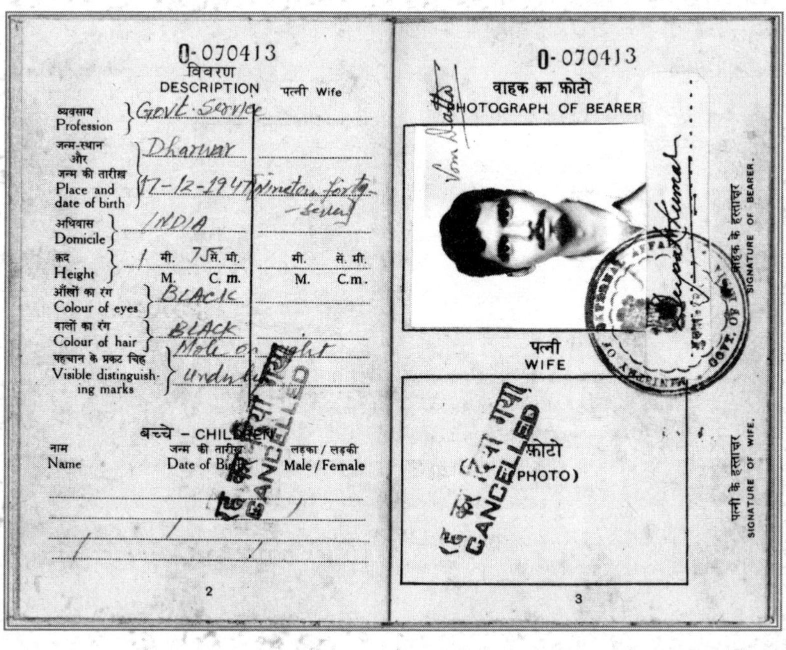

सत्यमेव जयते

VISIT OF
THE PRIME MINISTER
OF INDIA.

NAME Sh. D. R. Haldankar NO. 112

CABIN

Cabin Baggage Tag for Suitcase

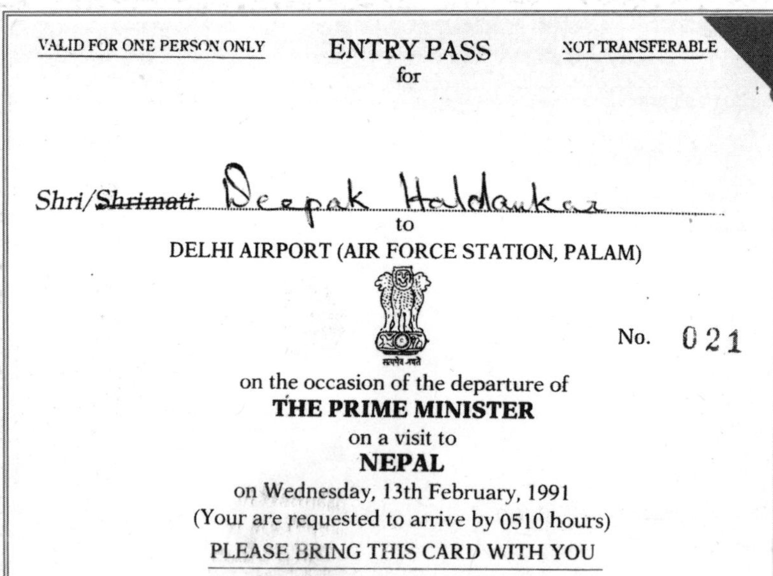

VALID FOR ONE PERSON ONLY — ENTRY PASS for — NOT TRANSFERABLE

Shri/~~Shrimati~~ Deepak Haldankar

to

DELHI AIRPORT (AIR FORCE STATION, PALAM)

सत्यमेव जयते

No. 021

on the occasion of the departure of
THE PRIME MINISTER
on a visit to
NEPAL
on Wednesday, 13th February, 1991
(Your are requested to arrive by 0510 hours)
PLEASE BRING THIS CARD WITH YOU

Delhi Airport Entry Pass

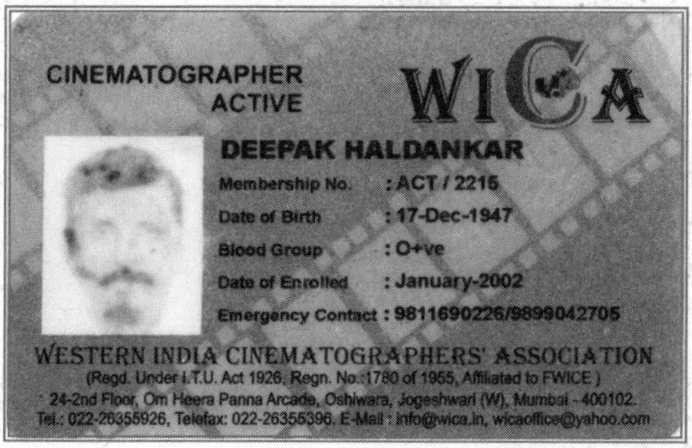

WICA Card

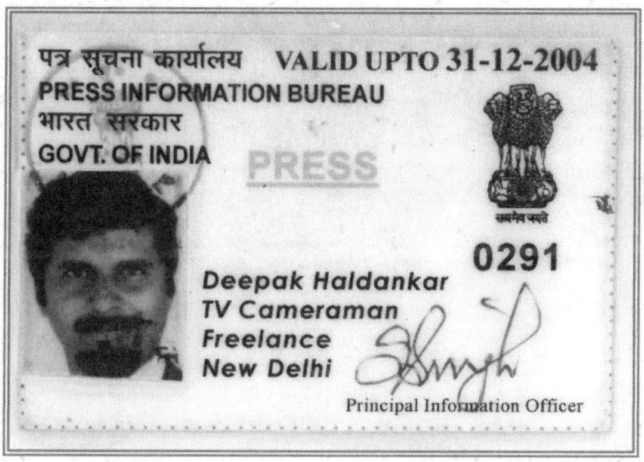

Press Information Bureau

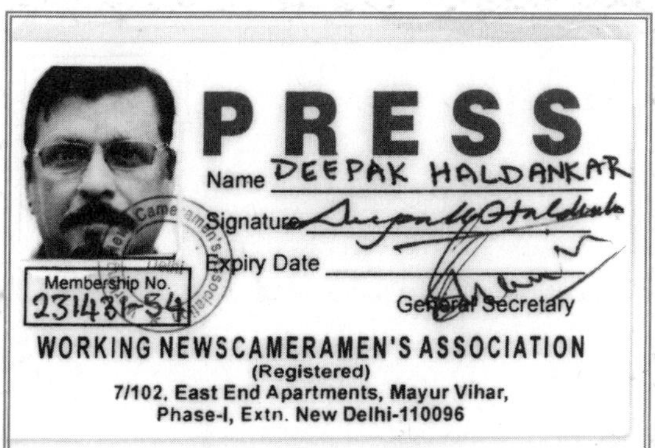

Press Information Bureau

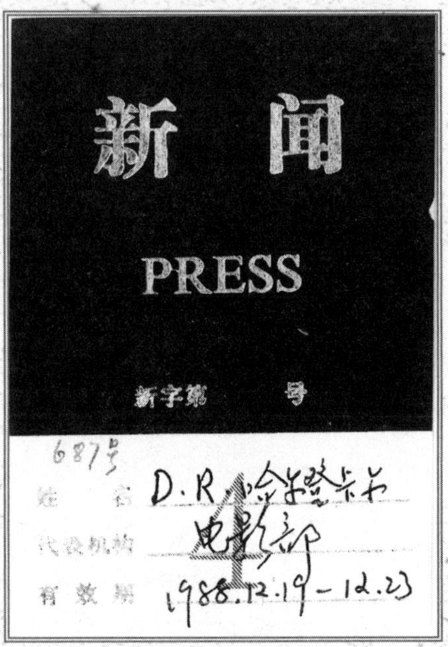

Press Card for China

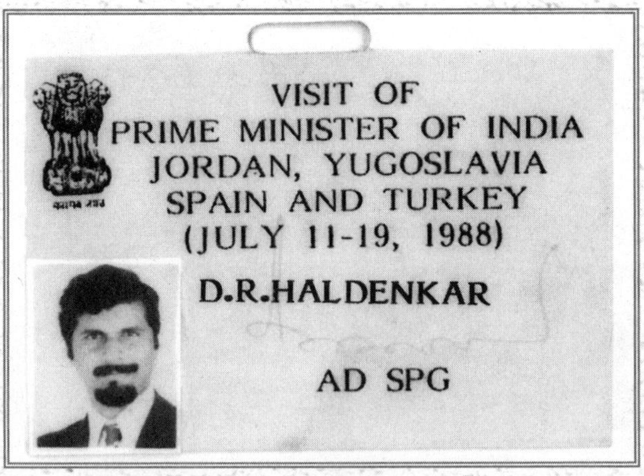

Travel ID Card for travelling with the Prime Minister

Royal Wedding Press ID

G-15 Press ID

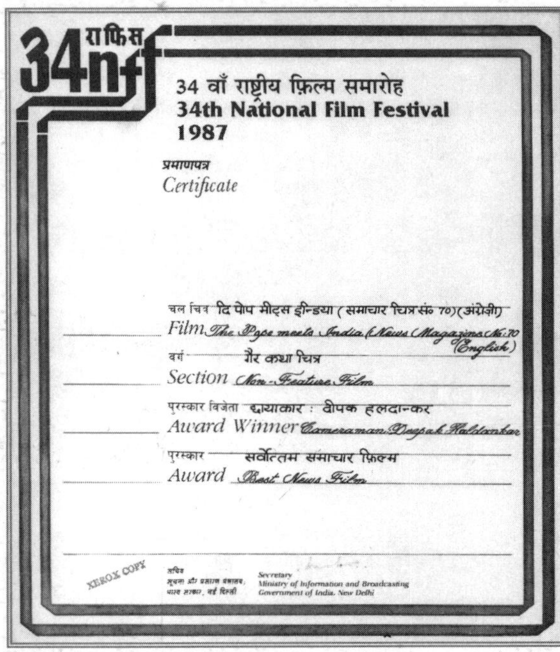

34nf राफिस

34 वाँ राष्ट्रीय फ़िल्म समारोह
34th National Film Festival
1987

प्रमाणपत्र
Certificate

चल चित्र दि पोप मीट्स इन्डिया (समाचार चित्र सं. 70) (अंग्रेज़ी)
Film The Pope meets India (News Magazine No. 70 (English)

वर्ग गैर कथा चित्र
Section Non-Feature Film

पुरस्कार विजेता छायाकार : दीपक हलदान्कर
Award Winner Cameraman Deepak Haldankar

पुरस्कार सर्वोत्तम समाचार फ़िल्म
Award Best News Film

XEROX COPY

सचिव
सूचना और प्रसारण मंत्रालय,
भारत सरकार, नई दिल्ली

Secretary
Ministry of Information and Broadcasting
Government of India, New Delhi

National Award for Pope Meets India—34th National Film Festival

Certamen Internacional de Cine Documental de Bilbao
Instituto Vascongado de Cultura Hispánica

EL FILME WHERE TIME STANDS STILL
de nacionalidad INDIA
dirigido por DEEPAK HALDANKAR

ha participado en el 20 Certamen Internacional de Cine Documental y Cortometraje celebrado en Bilbao (España), del 4 al 9 de Diciembre de 1978

Bilbao, 30 Diciembre de 1978

EL PRESIDENTE,

XEROX COPY

Where Time Stands Still—Bilbao

XV MIĘDZYNARODOWY FESTIWAL FILMÓW KRÓTKOMETRAŻOWYCH W KRAKOWIE

Kraków, 30. V. – 4. VI. 1978

DYPLOM UCZESTNICTWA
DIPLÔME DE PARTICIPATION

Dla filmu

WHERE TIME STANDS STILL

Reżyseria

DEEPAK HALDANKAR

Przewodniczący Komitetu Festiwalowego

MARIUSZ WALTER

Dyrektor Festiwalu

PIOTR SOKOŁOWSKI

XEROX COPY

Where Time Stands Still—Krakow

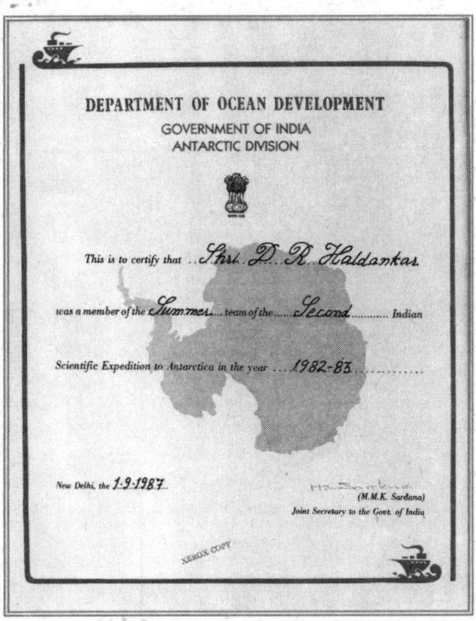

DEPARTMENT OF OCEAN DEVELOPMENT
GOVERNMENT OF INDIA
ANTARCTIC DIVISION

This is to certify that ..Shri. D. R. Haldankar

was a member of the Summer.... team of the......Second........... Indian

Scientific Expedition to Antarctica in the year ...1982-83............

New Delhi, the 1.9.1987.

(M.M.K. Sardana)
Joint Secretary to the Govt. of India

XEROX COPY

Antarctica- Department of Ocean Development

NATIONAL CADET CORPS

SENIOR DIVISION ARMY WING

CERTIFICATE "B"

INFANTRY

This is to certify that No. 337747 Rank L/CPL

Name HALDANKAR DEEPAK R s/o Shri, RAGHUNATH HALDANKAR

Unit 33 MAHARASHTRA BATTALION NCC

passed the Certificate "B" Examination held in FEBRUARY 1967, under the authority of THE MINISTRY OF DEFENCE, GOVERNMENT OF INDIA.

GRADING*

~~A (80% OR MORE MARKS)~~
~~B (65% TO 79% MARKS)~~
C (50% TO 64% MARKS)

*SCORE OFF GRADINGS NOT APPLICABLE

MINISTRY OF DEFENCE

GIPNLK—3/NCC Army/66—18-7-66—2,67,350

Lt Col

for *DIRECTOR GENERAL, NATIONAL CADET CORPS*

(JS DHALIWAL)

Certificate received by National Cadet Corps—33 Maharashtra Battalion NCC

Dipak takes a dip before taking over the camera

PICTURE OF ADVENTURE

MEET DIPAK HALDANKAR...

Once Charlie Chaplin's wife, his severest critic, watching his film said, "Where does music come from on that remote island?" Chaplin replied, "Tell me where the camera comes from and I will tell you where the music comes from!"

Have you ever wondered how all those breathtaking adventures on rivers, oceans, mountains or skies were filmed?

There must have been, behind the adventure seekers, a man with a camera, braving just as much of the elements, hanging on, putting the moments into a film and giving it a stamp of permanence.

Someone like Dipak Haldankar. The young man with a movie camera in his hands and adventure in his heart. He has been to the Antarctica with the Indian Expedition 1984, and also the aborted Indian Army Everest Expedition 1985.

Starting off as a lensman in Bombay, Dipak joined Films Division of India more

Dipak with the Bastar tribals: Time stood still

A camera, a man and the wilderness: in Antarctica

Picture of Adventure—*The Sun* magazine, December 1985

Face to face with death

Hindustan Times Correspondent

NEW DELHI, April 10 — A seven-member team which had gone to rescue four stranded members of the Army's recent Ganga-82 rafting expedition from Uttarkashi to Hardwar, had a near-encounter with a panther in the jungle but kept it at bay by shouting loudly and starting a fire of twigs.

The successful expedition, led by Maj. D. N. Das of the Army Service Corps, covered a distance of 207 kms on the narrow river from March 16 to April 7. Four inflated rubber rafts carrying two drivers, each, took part in the adventure. There was support from ground party keeping a watch on the rafts from the road running along the river.

Mr Deepak Haldankar, a newsreel officer of the Films Division, who took part in the expedition and filmed it, was a member of the rescue team. Narrating the story, he said by March 29, the expedition had gone through a number of mishaps and had lost two of its rafts in strong currents.

Between Gomateshwar and Devaprayag, the occupants of the remaining two rafts encountered a big boulder and tried to take their rafts across with the help of ropes. The latter gave way and the rafts were taken along by the current.

If the four — Maj. Das, Maj. Mohan, Lt. Patil and Sep. Biswas — had landed themselves on the side of the road, things would not have been difficult. But they were on the other side, which was all rocks, bushes and jungle. Not only that, Maj. Das tried to chase his raft and got separated from his companion, Sep. Biswas. The other two were together but had no knowledge of Maj. Das and Sep. Biswas being stranded like them.

The ground party had watched the mishaps, but no rescue teams could go across at that point because of the strong current. So the two teams of three persons and seven persons which left on foot to trace them could only cross the river over a bridge at Devaprayag.

The second team of seven persons included a local police sub-inspector and a civilian. It was around 6 p.m. and getting dark. After walking upwards about 10 km with the help of flashlights, the party located none of the stranded members. Instead, they heard the sound of a panther and the police official said the animal was around.

Slowly, the sound became louder and the seven men did not know from which direction they would be face to face with the deadly beast. Suddenly, Mr Haldankar gave a loud shout. All others followed him and the team made loud noises.

The sub-inspector, who had no weapon with him lighted a matchstick and put the dried bushes on fire. Even the lungi of the civilian was put in the blaze. That went on for two hours and a perplexed panther withdrew from the area, to much relief of the seven. Around 8 p.m., the team started retreating and reached Devaprayag around midnight.

It was only around 5 a.m. that the first three-member team could locate Maj. Mohan, Lt. Patil and Sep. Biswas. Maj. Das, who had spent the night in a cave, was traced later in the day.

There were a number of incidents during the expedition in which the rafts capsized and were retrieved after long distances. In one instance, Capt. N. K. Shrivastav was carried away under his upturned raft for nearly 300 metres. In another case, Maj. Mohan fell off his raft and was pushed along in the rapid current for five or six kilometres.

Near Tehri, all the four rafts capsized and Capt. (Dr) J. J. Faleiro and Lt. Anil Puri had their collar bones dislocated and later set right at Tehri Hospital.

While filming the spectacular scene of the rafts crossing, the confluence of Bhagirathi and Alaknanda at Devaprayag, Mr Haldankar slipped from a rock. His bag containing film and other equipment fell into the river and he was taken as drowned by some locals.

He was, however, clinging to some bushes on a cliff and was rescued when he shouted for help. Within an hour of this incident, Mr Haldankar was back at his job, filming the event!

Gurdwara men g

NEW DELHI, April 10 (UNI) — Tension prevails in the Shiv Nagar area of West Delhi here, following alleged forcible occupation of a commercial plot by a band of nearly 300 persons, including armed Nihangs, led by a former municipal councillor.

The land-grabbers include women and children. They claim that the plot belonged to a gurdwara in the area, but police say "the occupation is illegal."

A huge police force is keeping a round- ... vigil at the ...

HINDUSTAN TIMES 11th APRIL -82

Face to Face with Death—*Hindustan Times*, 11 April 1982

ter Sayeeda Khan.

singers

stan

rvedi

Haldankar—adventurous film maker

By Derek Bose

BRAINS and brawn rarely mix. And, in cinema profession, it is rarer still to find someone who combines his art with the adventure of scaling the lofty peaks of the Himalayas, journeying upstream Ganges, filming the Kenyan wild life, exploring Antarctica and investigating the tribal life of Bastar.

Deepak Haldankar has done all that—and more. But then, in our misplaced emphasis on patronising feature films, very little is either known or seen of his documentaries despite the fact that today, he is one of the most accomplished and respected professionals with few peers in international cinema.

"I guess I am the only Indian capable of the monkey tricks in adventure filming", he boasts with reason. "I am also the only one to have exposed as much footage to encircle the moon twice."

At 37, Haldankar is perfectly fit to take up the most challenging assignments. He is known for his ability to hold the camera rock steady whether filming in the midst of riotous street mobs, an unruly football match, a VIP reception at the airport, a public meeting or while shooting from an open aircraft.

"While covering the Everest assault last year with Bachendri Pal, I wanted to take an aerial shot of the peak during the early hours of the morning", he relates. "I took off in a Pillatus Spot aircraft with Captain Wig on the controls and flew at an altitude of 30,000 ft. with all the doors and windows open. It was a risky affair, partially because it was against the principles of aerodynamics and more so, as the vibrations from the aircraft could set a landslide down the mountain slopes. I did it because that was the only way to capture some unique shots of the Everest".

Deepak Haldankar

Haldankar considers that expedition the most strenuous in his career. Despite his experience of high altitude shooting in Ladakh, Chumetang and Lake Penninsaw, he felt thoroughly exhausted is the time the team reached the base camp at 19,000 ft. Moreover, the kind of noodles, unspiced boiled beans and tinned food stuff served "did not agree" with him. Ultimately, it was plain courage and determination that helped him complete the expedition successfully.

However, to this enterprising young man, no experience could be as memorable as the historic second Antarctica Expedition, which set sail from Goa on December 1, 1982. Haldankar was commissioned by the Department of Ocean Development to make a 20 minute 35 mm colour documentary, recording India's 110 day stay on the ice continent.

"Actually the priority of the expedition was not to shoot films, but to set up a station on Antarctica in as shot a time as possible", Haldankar explains. "At every stage, I had to literally quarrel, cajole and convince the scientists about the importance of a particular shot or sequence..."

For instance, there is an interesting blizzard scene in the film **"Exploration Antarctica"**, which Haldankar was specifically dissuaded from shooting. With the wind velocity over 100 km. p.h. and temperatures dipping to

Continued on page 21

reases

rrespondent

16—There ent in the position, actual figures from April released by try here to-

Haldankar—an adventurous film maker

Continued from page 17

minus 22 degrees Celsius, it was "humanly impossible to even take a peak shot from under a tent". Eventually, he settled for panning the sequence on zoom from a distant outpost.

Another dispute emanated when Haldankar insisted on filming from a huge glacier. "While I was busy convincing the leader of the expedition, Captain Raina, the glacier just disappeared into the sea...in two seconds flat!" From that moment, Haldankar had ever been so obedient to Captain Raina, for saving his life.

Opportunity, however, did come for Haldankar to prove his gratitude. He remembers noticing at Dakshin Gangotri—about 100 kms from the base camp—that the fuel means for snow scooters were inadvertently filled into the tanks of helicopters. Had he not alerted the naval pilots then, the helicopters would have exploded immediately on take off.

In fact, Haldankar entered into adventure filming in 1979, after ten years of covering news events and Government functions for Films Division. He was then asked to accompany the Ganga-Jamuna hovercraft expedition led by Dr Posseial of France — a 160 km stretch upstream to Uttarkashi.

In 1981, he covered the 425-km Jamuna expedition on rubber craft from Dak Pathar to Delhi. A year later, he was assigned the most challenging expedition of his career—the 207-km Uttarkashi-Haridwar stretch, up a gradient of 2000 ft. in "waters more turbulent than the Colorado".

Twice the rafts capsized. Haldankar recalls: "At Tehri, the Bhagirathi is joined by the Billanghana river, which once again enters a gorge upto Devprayag. The water of the river is increased by about a third and this adds to the turbulence, making the water gush through this narrow gorge, which at times is only 10 metres wide".

Traversing this portion of the river, proved to be most treacherous. Apprehending a calamity, Haldankar had positioned himself with his camera on a distant boulder, before two rafts capsized and the crew were thrown into the gushing rapids. While his colleagues struggled for life and expensive equipment flowed away downstream, Haldankar stayed put filming the entire sequence with clinical detachment. He did not even throw a rope to Captain Das (the leader of the team) when he signalled frantically for help.

Fortunately, there were no casualties, but the incident did foul up relations with the rest of the crew. Nevertheless, he participated in subsequent rescue operations and at one stage, he was instrumental in driving away a panther that had attacked the party. He shot that sequence too, but lost those reels in another accident later.

"We had nearly reached the end of our voyage at the historic confluence of Bhagirathi and Alaknanda when the accident occured", he recalls. "In my enthusiasm to shoot the closing scenes, I slipped and fell into the swirling waters below. My first concern was my camera slung around my neck and in desperation, clung on to the nearest ledge of rock... helplessly watching my equipment and rawstock washed away. If it were not for some locals who had assembled to witness our expedition, probably I to would have been carried away downstream".

For all this "daredevilry", Haldankar is infinitely grateful to his mentor, Nariman Irani, the doyen among cinematographers for having gromed him in the profession. He assisted the latter in films like "Talaash" and subsequently, helped Joe D'Souza in the all time Goan hit, **"Mouji Gorakarum"**. Then diverting to shorts, he made some notable documentaries like **"Arming the Mountains"** (on the Border Security Force), **"The Flying Sikh"** (on Milkha Singh), **"Just in Time'** (on cancer prevention and cure), besides covering international events like President Tito's funeral in Belgrade and Prince Charles' wedding in London.

Right now, he is preparing to film the Indian Expedition to South Pole this November. Meanwhile, he also hopes to attain his lifetime ambition of undertaking a voyage up River Narmada — notorious for its turbulent currents and crocodiles—from Jabalpur to Broach.

Modernisation schemes for

Haldankar—An Adventure Filmmaker—*Hindustan Times*, 17 May 1985

SCREEN, AUGUST 6, 1993, PAGE 17

DEEPAK HALDANKAR

The world is his playground

SPOTLIGHT

From the swirling sand dunes of the Thar to the rarified heights of the Himalayas and thence to the freezing environs of the Antarctic, cinematographer Deepak Haldankar has made the world his plavground.

DEEPAK Haldankar's is neither a name nor a face that will ring too many recognition bells. That's quite understandable considering the fact that Deepak Haldankar has spent the most memorable moments of his life behind the cine-camera, capturing for eternity some of those very memorable moments. Many of those 'expedition-to ...' documentaries - ranging from his earliest work for the Defence ministry (in '70) to his latest hovercrafting up the. Ganga (in 89) - are the result of his handiwork. The feather in his cap is, naturally the second Indian scientific expedition to the Antarctic in 1983.

Deepak wasn't always an adventure film cameraman. He started off his career in the late '60s as an assistant to Nariman Irani - "he is my guru", he says - and then went on to assist Anwar Siraj, too. He was the cinematographer for O.P Ralhan's 'Talaash'. The aim was to turn an independent cinematographer, but the field was too big and there were already too many big players cranking their wares. So Deepak thought that a change of milieu was essential if he was to make a name for himself. So he joined the News Services department of the Films Division.

In the early '70s there was no such thing as adventure photography. There were, naturally, no specialised cameras for shooting adventure sports such as river rafting, scuba-diving, para-sailing, aerial free-falling or even mountaineering. Nevertheless, when the Defence ministry wanted to do a study-documentary on *Arming The Mountains* in Leh, Haldankar was chosen for the job. He was then repeated for another Defence ministry sponsored documentary called *Characteristics of Mountain Terrain*. And with that Deepak had arrived.

Not only was Deepak soon considered a pioneer in the field of adventure photography, he soon established a name for himself as an innovative and resourceful photographer. One project followed another. Major among these were the three river rafting expeditions - two on the Ganga in '83 and in '87 with a French team lead by Dr. Michel, and the last, an army expedition under Maj. Das along the Yamuna. With recognition came rewards, too. The crowning glory - the expedition to the Antarctic - fetched him numerous awards including a special mention in the national film festival in 87. "The only reason why I did not get an national award was because in '87 adventure photography wasn't a separate category then. All awards were clubbed together in the general category. But the film did bag an international award; at a French festival.

The Antarctic expedition, needless to say, posed as many challenges as it was thrilling and exciting. Firstly the camera has to be 'winterised', a process that is the technological opposite of 'tropicalised'. The camera had also to be customised, in that everything from the eye-piece to the lens had to be subjected to special treatment that would stop them from freezing up. Then there was also the question of logistic. The terrain and the location was in the least user-friendly. Many a time he had to helicopter and reconnoitre the area that he planned to capture on film for eternity. And that was also the time when he had the most dangerous and exciting moments of his career. One such incident that has left an indelible impression on his mind was when he asked his mission commander for permission to land on an ice-berg and film the passage of the ship. "I thought that it was a good idea. But the captain refused permission for using the helicopter. In retrospect that was a good decision because moments later the iceberg came crashing down. I had under estimated the mass and depth of that particular berg," Haldankar recollects.

While that was a hair-rising experience, Haldankar was also involved in preventing a certain disaster. He noticed that the wrong fuel was being filled into one of the army helicopters at their disposal. The fuel was quickly emptied and the right fuel used. "The pilot was surprised, and a little amused, that I could identify the fuel even though I didn't know the rudiments of flying. I didn't spoil his amusement by informing him that my knowledge of fuels came from working with the army on numerous occasions," says he with a wry smile.

Haldankar has gone on to photograph 200 docu-films besides directing and photographing another 60 and finally producing-directing-filming another 15. His next major expedition is to raft down the Nile with a joint Indo-American team

But that will take time, as he admits. "The logistics involved are too staggering to attempt anything in a hurry. But the expedition is certainly on." Haldankar himself is raring to go. The accidental tryst with adventure photography has self-admittedly changed him from a person who played safe to a cameraman who seeks out challenges. "I love challenging the unknown," he says with the conviction of a man who has truly found his calling.

Deepak Haldankar is currently head of the News Services division of Films Division at Delhi. And he is not averse to the idea of filming a serial or a feature film if the opportunity ever arises.

– Sandeep Belagajee

The World is His Playground—*Screen*, 6 August 1993

Face to Face

Adventure Cameraman Haldankar

"Perhaps I am the only Indian cameraman, capable of the 'monkey tricks' in adventure filming", says Deepak Haldankar, whose 20 minute *Exploration Antartica* is part of the Panorama package in the current Filmotsav.

Produced by Films Division for the Department of Ocean Development, the 35mm colour documentary records India's 110 day Second Antartica Expedition launched from Goa on December 1, 1982. Haldankar was the cameraman who "literally had to bulldoze" his way to stay on board with the crew.

"Actually the priority of the expedition was not to shoot films but to set up a station in as short a time possible on the Ice Continent", explains Haldankar. "At every stage I had to quarrel, cojole and convince the scientists about the importance of a particular shot or sequence..."

For instance, there is an interesting Blizzard scene in the film which Haldankar was specifically dissuaded from shooting. With the wind velocity over 100 km.p.h. and temperatures dipping to minus 22 degrees celsius, it was humanly impossible to even "take a peak shot from under the tent". Eventually, Haldankar settled for 'panning' the sequence on 'zoom' from a distant outpost.

Another dispute emanated when Haldankar insisted on filming from a glacier, the size of a multi-storeyed building. "While I was engaged in convincing the leader of the expedition, Captain Raina, the glacier just disappeared into the sea... in two seconds!" Ever since, he has been obedient to Captain Raina for saving his life.

Haldankar branched into adventure filmmaking in 1979 after ten years of covering news events for Films Division. He was then commissioned to accompany the *Ganga-Jamuna* hovercraft expedition led by Dr Pesseial of France—a 160 km stretch upstream to Uttarkashi.

In 1981, he covered the 425 km *Jamuna* expedition on rubber raft from Katta Pathar to Delhi. A year later, he was assigned the most difficult expedition in his life—the 207 km *Uttarkashi-Haridwar* stretch up a gradient of 2000 feet in "waters more turubulent than the Colorado".

Twice the rafts capsized. Recalls Haldankar: "On one occasion, the leader Captain Das, fell into the waters and was fighting for life. He waved at me in desperation, but instead of throwing a rope in his aid, I stayed put with my camera, filming the entire sequence".

The incident did spoil his relations with the rest of the crew. He, nevertheless, participated in the subsequent rescue operations and, at one stage, was instrumental in driving away a panther which had attacked the party. He shot that sequence too, but lost those reels in another accident, later.

For all his 'daredevilry' and achievments, Haldankar is an extremely modest person. At 36, he has exposed as much footage as "to encircle the moon once around". His sights are now on *Mount Everest*—the expedition he is to cover this summer.

Derek Bose

Name of paper: FESTIVAL NEWS
Published at: Bombay
Dated: 18th January 1984

Adventure Cameraman Haldankar—*Festival News*, 18 January 1984

IV MID-DAY, May 13, 1988

'Shooting' from the skies

By Our Correspondent

Specialisation has come to filming also. And one of the new vistas opening up for camermen is that of aerial filming.

Films Division cameraman Deepak Haldankar feels he has had the great advantage of learning the ropes of aerial filming through his long career in that Governmental unit.

Widely travelled in India and abroad, accompanying expeditions, adventure seekers, and VIPs, he has written India's history on celluloid. Haldankar has found aerial filming a source of great joy.

"For me it was an uphill task learning all about it. I had to pick up the ways, the finer points, watching foreign filmers, or thinking out ways, as I went along. I realised that aerial filming is a different ball game altogether. It is different from the usual filming in technique and input.

"Aerial filming is a science and an art. To adroitly capture the skies and the scenes below, as you float at high speed with your camera, often in suspension, often in the open door of an aircraft, miles above, wearing an oxygen mask, you have to be prepared," he said.

"I have talked to experts like Bill Cartwright, the American stunt photographer, who filmed the helicopter dogfights in **On Her Majesty's Secret Service**, the James Bond film. And I have had my own varied and exciting experiences over the years in the Films Division which have taught me how to innovate. I have flown over Everest, shooting the Himalayas, at times we did films for the I and B Ministry about Ladakh relief operations, or the aerial perspectives of the Antarctica expedition and there have been so many other occasions to test my skill in the skies."

Preparing to capture the glory of the Himalayas.

He realises that a cinematographer has to be a very healthy person. He has to be able to hang outwards, tied to a monkey belt, fastening him to the aircraft securely, holding the camera, fitted with special gadgets to keep it steady and well angled. "You have to be very fit, and have a lot of stamina. You can't afford to waste footage and there may not be any retakes. Your reflexes have to be very sharp to catch the best shots at the speed you fly, and, of course, you can't afford to suffer the mildest form of vertigo," he said.

Once he saved the day by pointing out that one of the helicopters in the Antarctica expedition was being given the wrong fuel. He laughed and said, "I think an aerial cameraman soon learns a lot about the G-Force, using of oxygen, aerodynamics and flying patterns. The worst enemy is vibration which has to be controlled through gadgets in the camera. And a steady hand, which is not easy."

Haldankar says there is great scope for aerial filming and the aerial camerman. He is very excited that Doordarshan has signed a contract with Pawan Hans for helicopters. He says, "Basically, the choppers will speed up the bringing back of news footage from different places. There is a lot of scope in gathering good shots from a helicopter.

"Then, aerial filming is of great use for town planning, forest surveys, wildlife preservation surveys, pipe laying, and traffic planning."

And, of course, the Bombay film industry could wake up to the fact that they should use aerial filming for authentic shots of their ubiquitous monoplanes and helicopters sequences. In other countries there is so much scope for aerial stunt photography, for shooting scenes in the skies for war films and documentaries or TV films. Often, a dirigible, like the Goodyear Blimp, which is silent, is used to cover big events.

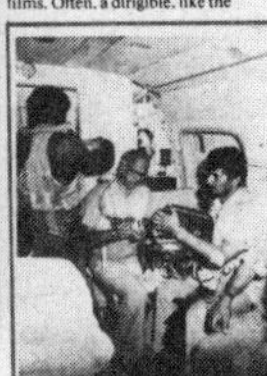

Deepak Haldankar (right) with his crew in a copter.

Haldankar's future looks bright, being India's most experienced aerial photographer. Thanks to the rigorous training programmes he is put through on and off before accompanying the high adventure sports and mountaineering or Antarctica expeditions, he is very fit and strong.

Shooting from the Skies—*Mid-Day*, 13 May 1988

IN FOCUS

READY.

No matter how challenging the assignment, this daredevil news and documentary film cameraman is on the move. He has trekked with an Everest team, gone to Antarctica and is now on to aerial photography

In Antarctica for the 2nd Expedition

DIPAK HALDANKAR

AIM.

In 1982, a dangerous river-rafting expedition from Uttar Kashi to Haridwar by the Indian Army came face to face with death. The expedition leader, Major B.N. Das, was flung out of the hovercraft into the chilling waters. He screamed for help pointing frantically at a rope lying on the shore. But the cameraman to whom he was bellowing, had his eye trained on the lens. In fact, when the mishap occurred, the photographer quickly positioned himself and began merrily filming the event, ignoring the appeals of help from Maj. Das.

Today, reflecting back on that misplaced enthusiasm, the cameramen, Dipak Haldankar, muses, "Major Das and the other members were so furious with me that they stopped talking to me. Absolutely ashamed of myself, I volunteered to go on a rescue mission a couple of days later when three of the members who had fallen out of the raft, had to swim to the other shore." The rescue team ran into a panther. Haldankar, whose physical strength has been his plus point, exhibited his strong lung power, making the panther stop in his tracks. After that, they lit a fire with the brandy they were carrying and frightened off the beast. This delayed the rescue but exonerated Haldankar.

A senior news and documentary film lensman with the Films Division of India, Dipak Haldankar has an addiction for challenging assignments, and his exuberant personality reverberates with excitement at the thought of adventure. He covered the 1984 Army Expedition to Mount Everest, during which tragedy struck, killing Major Bahuguna and three others as they tried to reach the peak. After training for months with the group and camping with them, Haldankar returned with a heavy heart and film cans full of the great Himalayas and the images of forlorn memories of an expedition that had failed.

"Being a film-chronicler has its extreme emotional impact. I never feel like a spectator. After I finished a film on bride-burning, I lay awake at nights thinking of the charred women, their anguished parents and what the cruel parents-in-law had said. One bereaved father told me that when he went to get his daughter's body, the mother-in-law told me, 'Take

SHOOT.

SUNDAY MAIL, September 16-22, 1990

9

Ready AIM Shoot—*Sunday Mail*, September 1990

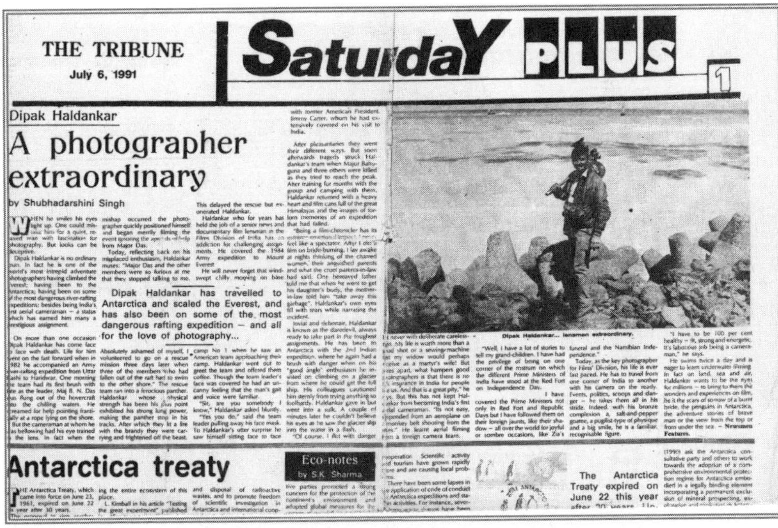

THE TRIBUNE

July 6, 1991

SaturdaY PLUS

1

Dipak Haldankar

A photographer extraordinary

by Shubhadarshini Singh

Dipak Haldankar has travelled to Antarctica and scaled the Everest, and has also been on some of the most dangerous rafting expedition — and all for the love of photography...

Dipak Haldankar... lensman extraordinary.

Antarctica treaty

Eco-notes

by S.K. Sharma

The Antarctica Treaty expired on June 22 this year

A Photographer Extraordinary—*The Tribune*, 6 July 1991

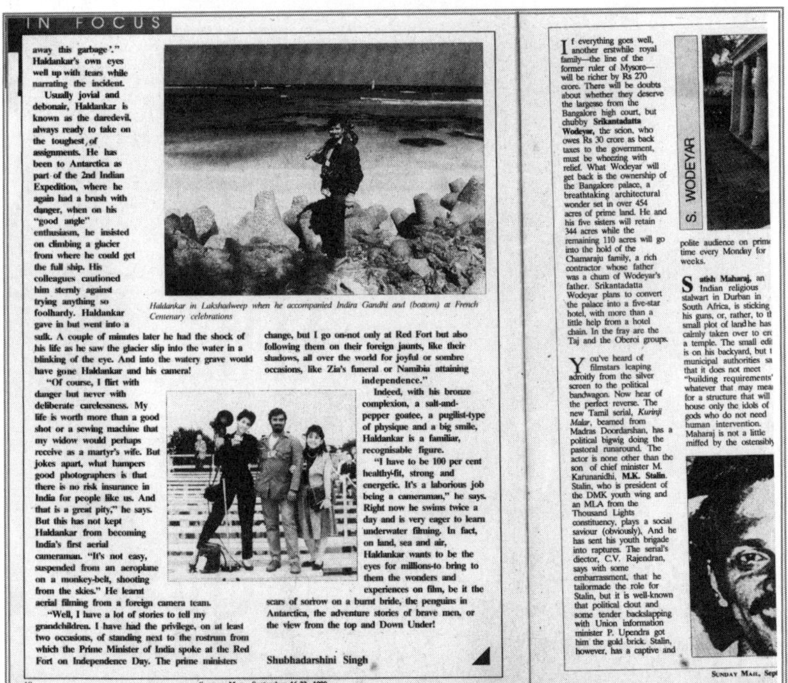

IN FOCUS

away this garbage'." Haldankar's own eyes well up with tears while narrating the incident.

Usually jovial and debonair, Haldankar is known as the daredevil, always ready to take on the toughest of assignments. He has been to Antarctica as part of the 2nd Indian Expedition, where he again had a brush with danger, when on his "good angle" enthusiasm, he insisted on climbing a glacier from where he could get the full ship. His colleagues cautioned him sternly against trying anything so foolhardy. Haldankar gave in but went into a sulk. A couple of minutes later he had the shock of his life as he saw the glacier slip into the water in a blinking of the eye. And into the watery grave would have gone Haldankar and his camera!

"Of course, I flirt with danger but never with deliberate carelessness. My life is worth more than a good shot or a sewing machine that my widow would perhaps receive as a martyr's wife. But jokes apart, what hampers good photographers is that there is no risk insurance in India for people like us. And that is a great pity," he says. But this has not kept Haldankar from becoming India's first aerial cameraman. "It's not easy, suspended from an aeroplane on a monkey-belt, shooting from the skies." He learnt aerial filming from a foreign camera team.

"Well, I have a lot of stories to tell my grandchildren. I have had the privilege, on at least two occasions, of standing next to the rostrum from which the Prime Minister of India spoke at the Red Fort on Independence Day. The prime ministers change, but I go on-not only at Red Fort but also following them on their foreign jaunts, like their shadows, all over the world for joyful or sombre occasions, like Zia's funeral or Namibia attaining independence."

Indeed, with his bronze complexion, a salt-and-pepper goatee, a pugilist-type of physique and a big smile, Haldankar is a familiar, recognisable figure.

"I have to be 100 per cent healthy-fit, strong and energetic. It's a laborious job being a cameraman," he says. Right now he swims twice a day and is very eager to learn underwater filming. In fact, on land, sea and air, Haldankar wants to be the eyes for millions-to bring to them the wonders and experiences on film, be it the scars of sorrow on a burnt bride, the penguins in Antarctica, the adventure stories of brave men, or the view from the top and Down Under!

Shubhadarshini Singh

Haldankar in Lakshadweep when he accompanied Indira Gandhi and (bottom) at French Centenary celebrations

10 SUNDAY MAIL, September 16-22, 1990

S. WODEYAR

If everything goes well, another erstwhile royal family—the line of the former ruler of Mysore—will be richer by Rs 270 crore. There will be doubts about whether they deserve the largesse from the Bangalore high court, but chubby **Srikantadatta Wodeyar**, the scion, who owes Rs 30 crore as back taxes to the government, must be wheezing with relief. What Wodeyar will get back is the ownership of the Bangalore palace, a breathtaking architectural wonder set in over 454 acres of prime land. He and his five sisters will retain 344 acres while the remaining 110 acres will go into the hold of the Chamaraju family, a rich contractor whose father was a chum of Wodeyar's father. Srikantadatta Wodeyar plans to convert the palace into a five-star hotel, with more than a little help from a hotel chain. In the fray are the Taj and the Oberoi groups.

You've heard of filmstars leaping adroitly from the silver screen to the political bandwagon. Now hear of the perfect reverse. The new Tamil serial, *Kurinji Malar*, beamed from Madras Doordarshan, has a political bigwig doing the pastoral runaround. The actor is none other than the son of chief minister M. Karunanidhi, **M.K. Stalin**. Stalin, who is president of the DMK youth wing and an MLA from the Thousand Lights constituency, plays a social saviour (obviously). And he has sent his youth brigade into raptures. The serial's director, C.V. Rajendran, says with some embarrassment, that he tailormade the role for Stalin, but it is well-known that political clout and some tender backslapping with Union information minister P. Upendra got him the gold brick. Stalin, however, has a captive and polite audience on prime time every Monday for weeks.

Satish Maharaj, an Indian religious stalwart in Durban in South Africa, is sticking to his guns, or, rather, to th[e] small plot of land he has calmly taken over to er[ect] a temple. The small edi[fice] is on his backyard, but t[he] municipal authorities sa[y] that it does not meet "building requirements" whatever that may mea[n] for a structure that will house only the idols of gods who do not need human intervention. Maharaj is not a little miffed by the ostensibly

SUNDAY MAIL, Sep[tember]

In Focus—*Sunday Mail*, September 1990

she, "I've always been surrounded by fabrics. Besides, both Nikhil and I love wearing cotton ourselves. So, I guess, it was only obvious that we start something ... at home. ... shoppers you see in the store, this strategy surely is working for this duo!

Besides cotton, travelling is another ... wife. She still continues to be my girl friend. And, I feel great!"

–Vishesh Prakash

Deepak Haldankar

Mountains, rivers, glaciers... he's conquered them all!

PRABHAS ROY

ON May 29, while the world was celebrating 50 years of man's ascent to Mt. Everest, this adventure film maker was reminiscing in his thoughts... the thoughts of his breathtaking adventures which he had filmed during his two expeditions to Mount Everest in 1984 and 1985. With a camera in his hand and adventure in his heart, 54-year-old Deepak Haldankar has filmed high adventures on rivers, oceans, mountains and skies. Widely travelled in India and abroad, accompanying expeditions, adventure seekers and VVIPs, this spirited filmmaker has written India's history on celluloid.

The two expeditions to Mount Everest which he filmed, are high points of his career in adventure filmmaking. In 1984, Deepak was part of the team that scaled Mt. Everest in which Bachendri Pal scaled the summit. "I filmed the entire expedition and my film got a national award," says Haldankar with a sense of pride.

And, if you thought that this was all that he's done, think again! He's not just filmed Everest from close quarters, he's filmed it from the skies too. Says Haldankar, "Shooting Mt. Everest from the skies was a great experience. Aerial filming is a great joy. But then, it is a different ball game. It is a science and an art. Capturing the skies and the scenes below as you float at high speed with your camera, often in suspension, often in the open door of an aircraft, miles above, wearing an oxygen mask is a great challenge."

Haldankar started off his career in the late 60s as a film cameraman. He was an assistant to Nariman Irani whom he considers his guru. However, lack of opportunities in Bollywood, forced Deepak to take up a job at the Films Division. Through his stint with Films Division, Haldankar had many great news stories and features to his credit. These include Rajiv Gandhi's visit to China, the first by an Indian Prime Minister after the 1962 war; Former President Sanjeeva Reddy at Prince Charles' wedding; the Pokhran blast; Atal Bihari Vajpayee's address to the UN; Namibia's freedom, and more. From Indira Gandhi to Atal Bihari Vajpayee, he has covered all the Prime Ministers hoisting the flag at Red Fort.

He's been there and pretty much done it all, but it is adventure filming which Haldankar cherishes the most. Besides Mount Everest, he has covered the Antarctica expedition, hovercraft and river rafting expeditions on the Ganga and Yamuna. He recalls one incident in Antarctica, when he faced stiff opposition from his team members because he insisted on filming from a glacier the size of a multi-storeyed building. "While I was engaged in convincing the team leader," he says smiling, "the glacier just disappeared into the sea in seconds!"

Haldankar has got plenty of rewards for his extraordinary filming skills. His film 'Exploration Antarctica' won an award at the Tulon Festival, France, while 'Gift of India' bagged international awards at Cannes, Warsaw, Bilboo, Lepizig. His short documentary on the tribals of Bastar, 'Where time stands still', was also among internationally acclaimed films.

Over 200 films, later, Haldankar is not sitting on past laurels. As a freelance film maker, he continues to bring innovations to his filming. Currently he is involved with a prestigious series 'Kalakaar Namaskar' (a tribute to the great master painters of India) for Doordarshan's international channel and DD Bharati.

–Vinod Behl

Mountains, Rivers, Glaciers: He Has Conquered Them All—Gurgaon Plus, 4 June 2003

Photographing Antarctica

Deepak Haldankar is a spirited young man who lives to face challenges. Not surprisingly, his list of photographic assignments reads like a tale of adventures. He has photographed more than 100 documentaries and shorts since he joined Films Division in 1970.

The kind of spirited young person he is, he has been associated with several 'risky' assignments that very few would volunteer for. His cinematographic adventures include photographing the tribal areas of Bastar; 'Ganga — 82' — an expedition which involved flowing with the waters of the river Ganga from Uttarkashi to Hardwar in boats; and his most recent one — 'Exploration Antarctica.'

We have pleasure in reproducing excerpts from an interview conducted with him recently by IPC's Rajesh Singh.

RS: Mr. Haldankar, will you tell us something about the Antarctica Expedition? What did it involve for you as a cinematographer?

DH: Well, 'Exploration Antarctica' was an important milestone in our country's scientific achievements. We had a team of scientists and experts from various disciplines who studied important aspects of its environment, giving us pioneer status in this field. My responsibility, as I saw it, was not only to record important activities, but to give my audience the thrill, the joy and the fear of being in those unknown lands.

RS: In Antarctica, as we understand, the conditions must be quite difficult. How did you cope with them?

DH: You are right. Because of low temperatures, even normal activities involved a great deal of effort. Breathing was difficult, the mental faculties tend to get dulled and there was an ever present danger of frostbite. Carrying equipment weighing more than 50 kg all alone meant taking oneself to the limits of endurance.

There was hardly anything that could be relied upon. Such was the effect of low temperature, that the nuts and bolts of my 'Arri' would come off and lenses would get repeatedly fogged. Also, constant use of special goggles for protection against ultraviolet light impaired visual judgement. These obstacles, especially the unreliability of equipment, certainly were a cause for nightmares!

RS: Cinematography under such extreme conditions must have required a lot of planning. What special precautions did you take?

DH: We did a lot of homework. Every effort was made to keep the equipment in working order. Every piece of equipment was treated with special antifog grease and subjected to rugged tests by my colleagues. I chose Arriflex 2C as my camera as I know it inside out. I had all the tools and the confidence of repairing the camera if anything went wrong.

Above all, I had carried with me at least one important item I could really take for granted — Eastman colour negative film, Type 5247. With all my worries regarding equipment and visual judgement under such harsh conditions, I depended a great deal upon the physical prowess and exposure latitude of 5247. And it proved me right.

RS: What exposure rating did you give to Eastman colour negative 5247? What are your reactions?

DH: I rated the film for 32 ASA with 85 N3 filter. Such was the intensity of light that I had to operate at f16 all the time. Still, I thought I was using some of the overexposure latitude of your film.

I am happy to say that ECN 5247 withstood the extremes very well indeed. On the physical aspect, the film did not become brittle and the results are quite steady on the screen — a remarkable feature.

By the way, I am very happy about the introduction of your high speed Eastman colour negative film. It will be most useful in the sort of coverage that I do.

Photographing Antarctica—Interview

I would like to express my heartfelt gratitude to Dr Anamika Sharma, Lecturer, EAP, Trinity College, University of Melbourne whose support, patience, and encouragement were invaluable throughout the writing process. Her thoughtful guidance and careful corrections enriched this work immensely. Your belief in my work gave me the confidence to keep going. This book carries a part of your kindness—Thank you